WORLD OF ART

This famous series
provides the widest available
range of illustrated books on art in all its aspects.
If you would like to receive a complete list
of titles in print please write to:
THAMES AND HUDSON
30 Bloomsbury Street, London WC1B 3QP
In the United States please write to:
THAMES AND HUDSON INC.
500 Fifth Avenue, New York, New York 10110

Printed in Singapore

MICHAEL ARCHER

Art
Since
1960

180 illustrations, 74 in color

THAMES AND HUDSON

For Petonelle

© 1997 Thames and Hudson Ltd, London

First published in the United States of America in 1997 by
Thames and Hudson Inc., 500 Fifth Avenue, New York, New York 10110

Library of Congress Catalog Card Number 96-61018
ISBN 0-500-20298-2

Printed and bound in Singapore

Contents

Preface

Anyone who looks carefully at the art of today will be confronted with a perplexing profusion of styles, forms, practices and agendas. From the outset, it appears that the more one sees, the less certain one can be about what allows works to be designated 'art' at all, at least from a traditional point of view. For one thing, there no longer seem to be any particular materials that enjoy the privilege of being immediately recognizable as the stuff of art: recent art has used not only oil paint, metal and stone, but also air, light, sound, words, people, food and much else besides in its making. There are few, if any, techniques and methods of working nowadays that can guarantee the finished object's acceptance as art. Conversely, it frequently appears that one can do little to prevent the outcome of even the most mundane activities from being misconstrued as art. Although painting may remain important for many, alongside traditional artists there are some who use photography and video, and others who engage in such varied activities as going for walks, shaking hands and cultivating plants.

In 1961 at the start of a decade in which all previous assumptions about art were to be put to the test, the philosopher Theodor Adorno opened his *Aesthetic Theory* with the following statement: 'Today it goes without saying that nothing concerning art goes without saying, much less without thinking.' Even the way in which art itself had been understood to constitute a challenge to the established social equilibrium was called into question. Just what it meant to describe something as modern or as avant-garde began to change. The richness and diversity of contemporary art practice is not, though, symptomatic of a chaotic state of affairs; certain major themes reveal themselves in a study of the art of the past forty years. In particular, artists have re-examined some of the gestures of the modernist avant-garde made earlier in the century and have reinterpreted them and carried them forward.

What follows is one attempt at a partial survey of the profound changes that have occurred in the art of Europe and the US from the beginning of Pop art onwards. Broadly chronological in its treatment of the subject, this book uses a small number of major themes to examine the huge variety of forms and practices that have appeared since then.

A renewed consideration of the relationship between art and everyday life connects the apparently very different works associated with Pop and Minimalism. Exploring the shared concerns behind these two tendencies provides an understanding of the wide range of post-Minimal work that included Conceptualism, Land art, Performance and Body art and the beginnings of Installation. All of this work of the 1960s challenged the modernist account of art history most particularly identified with the US critic Clement Greenberg. A consequence of this challenge was the recognition that the meaning of an artwork did not necessarily lie within it, but as often as not arose out of the context in which it existed. This context was as much social and political as it was formal, and questions of politics and identity, both cultural and personal, were to be central to much art of the 1970s. Prime among the factors then, and something that has been of lasting significance, was the impact of feminist theory.

Psychoanalytic, philosophical and other cultural theories became increasingly important towards the end of the 1970s in the formulation of a critical postmodernism. The work which these theories were used to interpret continued the questioning of the nature of art that had begun in the 1960s. Alongside this, however, was a resurgence of broadly traditional painting, which, viewed at the time as a largely conservative reaction to the experiments of the 1960s and 1970s, was supported by the explosion of the art market during the financial boom of the 1980s.

The final chapter of the book looks at the works in, and the curatorial rationale behind, a number of influential exhibitions mounted during the last decade. In so doing it examines the ways in which the themes and preoccupations of the preceding years are carried forward and transformed in current art.

CHAPTER ONE

The Real and Its Objects

At the beginning of the 1960s it was still possible to think of works of art as belonging to one of two broad categories: painting and sculpture. Cubist and other collages, Futurist performance and Dadaist events had already begun to challenge this simple duopoly, and photography had increasingly been making strong claims for recognition as an art medium. Nonetheless, the notion persisted that art essentially comprised those products of human creative endeavour that we would wish to call painting and sculpture. In the years since 1960 there has been a breaking down of the certainties of this system of classification. To be sure, some artists still paint and others make what tradition would refer to as sculpture, but these practices now take their place among a far wider range of activities.

A new magazine, *Artforum*, appeared on the West Coast of America in 1962. In tongue-in-cheek manner it made its position clear by giving pride of place in the first issue to a statement by Lester D. Longman, Chairman of the Department of Art at the University of California, on the occasion of the opening of a survey exhibition, 'The Art of Assemblage', at the Museum of Modern Art, New York. Over five pages Longman investigated and rejected much that is now notorious in the art of that time: the 'action painting' of Jackson Pollock (1912–56); the large paintings of Barnett Newman (1905–70), monochrome but for one or two thin stripes running down them; the blue canvases executed with a roller, or the performances involving nude women as 'paintbrushes' of Yves Klein (1928–62); the 'combines', such as *Bed* (1955), wall-mounted bedclothes smeared with paint, or *Monogram* (1959), a stuffed goat ringed with an old tyre, of Robert Rauschenberg (b. 1925); the sculptures of crushed car bodies by César (b. 1921); the mechanized junk sculptures of Jean Tinguely (1925–91) – one of which, *Homage to New York* (1960), had famously self-destructed in the gardens of New York's Museum of Modern Art in 1960 – and the Happenings of Allan Kaprow (b. 1927), Claes Oldenburg (b. 1929), Jim Dine (b. 1935) and Red Grooms (b. 1937). 2

1 (left) Robert Rauschenberg *Bed* 1955

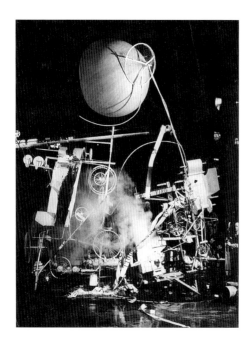

2 Jean Tinguely
Homage to New York 1960

Longman's objection to art of this kind was not that it existed, but rather that it seemed increasingly to be speaking for mainstream culture. He was right; it was. The work of Robert Rauschenberg and Jasper Johns (b. 1930) since the mid-1950s was referred to as neo-Dada because of its particular use of subject matter derived from the everyday world. Use of the term pointed less to the activities of Hugo Ball (1886–1927), Tristan Tzara (1896–1963) and others at the Cabaret Voltaire in Zurich in 1916, than to the work of the French artist Marcel Duchamp (1887–1968). Duchamp had invented the term 'readymade' to describe the mass-produced objects he chose, bought and subsequently designated as works of art. The earliest of these was *Bicycle Wheel* (1913), a bicycle wheel mounted on a stool; the most infamous, *Fountain* (1917), was a men's urinal signed 'R. Mutt'. With the readymade, Duchamp asked the viewer to think about what defined the uniqueness of the artwork among the multiplicity of all other objects. Was it something to be found in the artwork itself, or in the artist's activities around the object? These enquiries reverberate throughout the art of the 1960s and beyond.

There are two key ideas bound up in the word 'assemblage'. The first is that, however much the bringing together of certain images

3 Robert Rauschenberg
Buffalo II 1964

and objects might produce art, those images and objects never quite lose their identification with the ordinary, everyday world from which they were taken. The second is that this connection with the everyday, if one is unashamed of it, gives one free rein to use a wide range of materials and techniques not hitherto associated with the making of art. In the mid-1950s, Jasper Johns made a painting of the US flag, *Flag* (1954–55). The painting is certainly a picture of a commonplace object and symbol, but it can also be seen as a formal arrangement of colours, lines and geometric shapes. What is more, the flag in reality, consisting of colours on a piece of cloth, is no more substantial, three-dimensional and object-like than Johns's painting. The same was true of the targets he subsequently painted. At the beginning of the 1960s, following his 'combine' paintings, Rauschenberg produced a series of canvases containing a variety of silk-screened images as well as drawn and painted marks. These images were taken not only from the history of art, but also from the media. Just as images recur constantly in newspapers, magazines, and in one TV bulletin after another, so do elements in Rauschenberg's paintings. John F. Kennedy's repeated hand in *Buffalo II* (1964), for example, sets up a rhythm across the canvas quite unlike the compositional effects of earlier art.

4

The impulses evident in this work of the later 1950s – an interest in the ordinary, a willingness to embrace chance (not only a legacy of Dada, but also a recognition that in life things just happen) and a new sense of the visual – each led art in two directions: towards Pop and towards Minimalism. Outwardly, work associated with one of these movements seems to share little ground with the other. What do a screenprint of Marilyn Monroe by Andy Warhol (1928–87) and an arrangement of square copper plates on the floor by Carl Andre (b. 1935) have in common? The artists and critics of the time, though, were in no doubt whatsoever that much was shared between the two.

Pop art appeared and was acknowledged as a movement in the US at the very beginning of the 1960s. By 1962, it was possible to identify a common sensibility among a number of artists, notably Roy Lichtenstein (b. 1923), Andy Warhol, Claes Oldenburg, Tom Wesselman (b. 1931), and James Rosenquist (b. 1933), all of whose work used subject matter drawn from the banality of urban America. In a significant departure from the emotionally charged styles of the Abstract Expressionists, moreover, the work of these artists also appeared to be dependent upon the techniques of mass visual

4 (left) Jasper Johns
Flag 1954–55

5 (right) Roy Lichtenstein
*I Know How You Must Feel,
Brad* 1963

culture. Lichtenstein, for example, selected individual frames from cartoon strips, altering them slightly to suit his purposes, and reproduced these on a large scale in oil on canvas. The process of replication, though, was not inventive, free or playful, but precise and closely observed. Instead of interpreting the comic strip in the expansive, painterly way that Abstract Expressionism had led people to expect, Lichtenstein produced laboriously, by hand, a simulation of the screened dot technique by means of which the original strip had been printed. Because the result was so dry and 'unemotional', it was possible to believe that there had been no interpretation at all. His paintings looked, at first glance, as mechanically fashioned as their source material, although it is evident in a painting like *I Know How You Must Feel, Brad* (1963) that the idea of art as an emotionally expressive activity is being ironically considered.

At the end of 1962, a symposium on Pop art was held at the

Museum of Modern Art in New York. One of the contributors, the critic Henry Geldzahler, commented: 'The popular press, especially and most typically *Life* magazine, the movie close-up, black and white, technicolour and wide screen, the billboard extravaganzas, and finally the introduction, through television, of this blatant appeal to our eye into the home – all this has made available to our society, and thus to the artist, an imagery so pervasive, persistent and compulsive that it had to be noticed.' The ensuing discussion, representative of the general questioning of this new art, concentrated on whether Pop had contributed something new in terms of either form or content. Those who wished to play down its originality pointed out that there seemed to be no innovations of form that had not already been tried by Jasper Johns or the Abstract Expressionists. The tinned spaghetti, for example, which appears as a sort of artistic trademark in paintings such as *I Love You With My Ford* (1961) and the later, huge *F-111* (1965), both by James Rosenquist, refers back to the dripped swirls and skeins of paint in Jackson Pollock's work. Likewise, Andy Warhol's repetition of motifs – soup tins, Coke bottles, money, news photos, famous people – borrows a means of covering the canvas used by Johns in his alphabet and number paintings. In Johns's case this was a solution to the problem – which originated in Abstract Expressionism – of painting with equal emphasis all over the canvas, instead of in the centre where the main subject would normally appear and supportively round the edges. Using a number sequence starting in the top left-hand corner and finishing in the bottom right was a suitable system for achieving the desired
7   result. By 1962, as in *Do-It-Yourself (Flowers)*, Warhol had ironically outdone Johns by making canvases of the outlined scenes found in children's Painting by Numbers kits.

   For Warhol, repetition was also bound up much more fundamentally with the way we see and treat other kinds of images and objects. His first exhibition, at the Ferus Gallery in Los Angeles in 1962, was of 32 paintings of individual Campbell's Soup cans propped up on a narrow ledge running around the walls. Subsequent paintings with multiple images of soup cans, Coke bottles, savings stamps and money reiterated the idea of works of art as commodities.
8   This idea was further strengthened in 1964 by his stacks of *Brillo Boxes*, an exhibition at Leo Castelli's gallery that covered the walls with a repeated flower image, and another at the Stable Gallery which filled the space with reproduction Campbell's Tomato Juice boxes. Later, for his 1966 Castelli show, Warhol 'redecorated' the

6 James Rosenquist *F-111* 1965

space with *Cow Wallpaper*. From 1963 onwards, he was also making films. With their use of a fixed camera, lack of narrative structure and excessive length, *Sleep* (1963: a man sleeping) and *Empire* (1964: a static shot of the Empire State Building) established a new relationship between real- and film-time, while investigating the quality of attention paid by an audience when confronted with imagery.

In a 1963 interview, Warhol commented on his preoccupation with imagery associated with death. Tabloid disaster pictures, road crash victims, the electric chair, race riots, North America's most wanted criminals, the recent suicide of Marilyn Monroe, the bereavement of Jackie Kennedy, and Elizabeth Taylor (who was reported to be very ill at the time he began to use her face) were all images which dwelt upon the theme of death: 'It was Christmas or Labor Day – a holiday – and every time you turned on the radio they said something like, "4 million are going to die." That started it. But when you see a gruesome picture over and over again, it doesn't really have any effect.' A story covered by every bulletin of the day, reported in all the newspapers and analysed in all the magazines soon loses its immediacy and starts to be absorbed by the systems of

7 Andy Warhol (above) *Do-It-Yourself (Flowers)* 1962

8 (right) Andy Warhol *Brillo Boxes* 1964

communication through which it is made available. The news and the media by which it is delivered are ubiquitous and egalitarian. Warhol's famous statements – that he wanted to be a machine, that in the future everyone will be famous for fifteen minutes, that we all drink Coke and no amount of money will get the US president a better bottle than the one being drunk by the bum on the street

corner – are all reflections of this. To emphasize his recognition that art could not escape being treated as a commodity in the same way as tins of soup, soap pads and boxes of cereal, Warhol dubbed his studio 'The Factory', and described the way his assistants helped with the multiple screen-printing of the images he selected as similar to a production line. As with Lichtenstein, though, this apparent anonymity of execution was largely an act. Warhol's decisions on which image and what colours to use, and even how, precisely, to introduce mistakes into the screening process, were crucial.

As far as the subject matter of Pop art went, its banality was itself an affront to its critics. Without clearer evidence that the material had undergone some sort of transformation on being incorporated into art, the art itself could not be said to offer anything that life did not already provide. Against this opinion, Lichtenstein was quite clear that transformation was not art's function anyway: 'Transformation is a strange word to use. It implies that art transforms. It doesn't, it just plain forms.'

Pop's formal references to Abstract Expressionism emphasize the degree to which it continued to be art. In dialogue with its precursors it produced the necessary tension between generations, a simultaneous continuation of and reaction to that which had gone before. Somewhat as Pollock is recalled by Rosenquist's tinned spaghetti, the legacy of modern art is repackaged and offered anew by Lichtenstein. A series of 'Brushstrokes' from 1965, carefully and precisely executed, displayed Abstract Expressionism as a style, making obvious the fact that the expressiveness associated with it is not a transparent and absolute record of an emotional state, but a culturally specific set of signs by means of which that state is felt to be best represented.

In 1961, Claes Oldenburg turned his studio, which had once been a shop, back into a shop. He filled it with models of items of food and clothing made from muslin soaked in plaster over wire frames, painted in enamels in the expected colours but in a gloopy, loose, Abstract Expressionist way, and offered them for sale. Oldenburg had staged Happenings under the aegis of his Ray Gun pseudonym, and *The Store*, the shop that behaved like a shop, continued this approach. But it also brought issues of time passing and, more particularly, movement closer to the activity of sculpture. Lichtenstein's comic strips dealt with these as well, unfolding the closed narrative of the artwork into the flow of everyday life. The individual items offered for sale in Oldenburg's store became sculpture for him because of the

10

9 Roy Lichtenstein *Little Big Painting* 1965

way in which they were treated. People purchased them, took them home and behaved towards them as if they were pieces of sculpture. By the following year he was exhibiting stuffed vinyl and cloth replicas of a hamburger, a slice of cake and an ice cream cone. With the colour now in the material and no longer applied in dollops and dribbles of paint these new, 'cleaned up' sculptures looked to the conservative critic Sydney Tillim, 'too much like the things from which they derive'. That they were each the size of a person, or that the pair of blue trousers included in the same show would have fitted a giant, was apparently beside the point. For the more sympathetic, Oldenburg's experiments were startlingly innovative. The outer casings were sewn and then stuffed with kapok. Thus their form was built up from the inside, rather than as a result of traditional carving, or modelling over an armature, from the outside. Because of the lack

of rigidity in the materials, gravity ultimately decided the work's final form and not Oldenburg. In this sense the 'replicas' could be understood as things that were somewhat uncomposed. In addition, Oldenburg saw their softness bringing the problems of painting into sculpture. The effect is 'not a blurring (like the effect of atmosphere on hard form) but *in fact* a softening'.

Drawing the environmental expansiveness of Happenings back into art objects was achieved in other ways by Tom Wesselman. His early works were collages of photographs of the packets of food products found in magazine advertisements. Somewhat akin to the emblematic 1956 collage *Just What Is It That Makes Today's Homes So Different, So Appealing?* by the British artist Richard Hamilton (b. 1922), the consumer's dream-home interiors Wesselman created

10 (left) Claes Oldenburg *The Store* 1961 (interior view)

11 (below) Tom Wesselmann *Great American Nude No. 54* 1964

subsequently developed to become mixed media tableaux. Some of these, in his 'Great American Nude' series, for instance, were enlivened by the inclusion of taped sounds (*Great American Nude No. 54*: 1964), and a radio or an attached telephone ringing intermittently. Another work, *Bedroom Tit Box* (1968–70), even required the presence of a model's naked breast. Tableaux were also made by George Segal (b. 1924) and Ed Kienholz (1927–94). Segal's humdrum scenarios – a café table, a launderette – were populated by life-size white plaster figures. The people in Kienholz's raw scenes – the bar in *Beanery* (1965), the brothel in *Roxy's* (1961), and *Back Seat Dodge-38* (1964) – were not plaster casts but robotic mannequins assembled from junk, scrap and cast-offs.

Kienholz was a West Coast artist, one of a number, including Mel Ramos (b. 1935), Billy Al Bengston (b. 1934), Wayne Thiebaud (b. 1920) and Edward Ruscha (b. 1937), working in a Pop idiom. Ramos and Thiebaud were painters, qualifying as Pop artists by virtue of their subject matter. Bengston's prints and canvases celebrated youth culture through their depictions of the motorcycle. Ruscha's interest lay in the architecture and signs of Los Angeles, the simple language and imagery of billboards, and the rectilinear

12 Ed Kienholz *Roxy's* 1961

13 Edward Ruscha *Los Angeles County Museum On Fire* 1965–68

lines of such commonplaces as gas stations. Robert Indiana (b. 1928), who adopted the name of his home state, took the visual style of his paintings from the conventions of roadside signs. The stark readability of their lettering and the demotic appeal of their imagery were used in designs whose brief messages both expressed and questioned the attitudes and character of contemporary America.

Pop art, as described so far, was a North American phenomenon: American in terms of those involved, insofar as it treated a kind of social reality, and in terms of viewing the quintessentially American world that went hand in hand with that reality. The name, Pop, though, was older, having been first used in connection with the work of the British artists Richard Hamilton, Eduardo Paolozzi (b. 1924), Nigel Henderson (1917–85), Peter Blake (b. 1932) and others in the 1950s. Their focus, too, had been US culture, although their treatment of it had necessarily been more distanced and reflective while embracing its products and implications. It was what the critic Thomas Hess called, in contrast to the vibrant openness of the US version, not just 'bookish', but actually looking 'as if made by librarians'. In the early 1960s another group of artists, most of them associated with London's Royal College of Art, started showing work which seemed closely connected, both in terms of subject matter and treatment. Richard Smith (b. 1931), Allen Jones (b. 1937), Derek Boshier (b. 1937), Peter Phillips (b. 1939), the American R. B. Kitaj (b. 1932), and David Hockney (b. 1937) all used figurative material culled from the media and from the streets of the cities around them. Kitaj had already begun to employ these techniques in his examination of the political and cultural legacies of twentieth-century history. Abstract passages in the paintings of Jones and Hockney brought them close to other contemporaries – particularly Paul Huxley (b. 1938) and John Hoyland (b. 1934) – who had been strongly influenced by the first showings in Britain of Abstract Expressionist works. Certain painting exhibitions at the time even stipulated a minimum size for submitted canvases and demanded, in concert with the insistence on flatness of the US Post-painterly Abstraction then current, that they should not project more than a certain distance from the wall. Hockney's paintings were noteworthy for their wilful mix of abstract and figurative elements, and for the manner in which they used the marks of graffiti and the language of teenage crushes in the expression of sexuality and desire. At a time before the relative easing of the proscriptive laws on homosexuality in Britain, Hockney was openly gay, and in *We Two Boys Together Clinging* and *The Most Beautiful Boy in the World*, both from 1961, he begins something which would be most persistently explored in his series of Californian swimming pool paintings of the mid-decade.

As in Oldenburg's *The Store*, a preoccupation with time and movement is evident in the rationale behind the multiple panels of Lichtenstein's *Whaam!* (1963), where the firing of the missile and its explosion are temporally distinct events, but in other instances mobility was more literally incorporated into the artwork. Kinetic art developed out of a general interest in Constructivism and a more particular interest in the early Kinetic pieces by Naum Gabo (1890–1977). Centred in Paris, particularly at the Galerie Denis René, it brought together a culturally diverse group of artists. Pol Bury (b. 1922) from France, the Israeli Agam (b. 1928), the Argentinian Julio Le Parc (b. 1928), Jesús Rafaël Soto (b. 1923) from Venezuela and the Swiss Jean Tinguely all produced works, motorized or otherwise, with moving parts. Soto's 'Vibration Structures', begun in the late 1950s, had developed an environmental scope by the end of the 1960s, as had *Cube of Ambiguous Space* (1969). Art of this kind, changing through time, was seen to have close connections with another variant which explored the degree to which pattern and colour could be used to create the illusion of movement. This was dubbed Op – short for Optical – art, an abbreviation which brought it into at least semantic proximity with Pop. Because of their concern with surface pattern, the paintings of Bridget Riley

15

15 (above) Jesús Rafaël Soto
Cube of Ambiguous Space 1969

16 (right) Victor Vasarely,
plate 2 from the portfolio
Planetary Folklore 1964

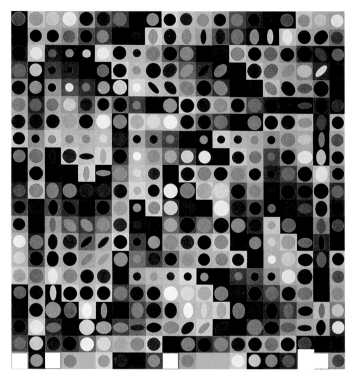

17 Bridget Riley *Twist* 1963

(b. 1931) in Britain, Paris-based Hungarian Victor Vasarely (b. 1908), Frenchman François Morellet (b. 1926) and Richard Anuszkiewicz (b. 1930) in the US, could be seen as a regression to that art obsessed with retinal sensation to the exclusion of all else so detested by Duchamp. The kind of unsettling effects produced by Vasarely's grids in *Planetary Folklore* (1964), for example, or the black-and-white lines of Riley's *Twist* (1963) or *Current* (1964), however, were more thoroughly physical than that. There was a somatic element in the viewing of Op art that would draw spectators to ground those illusions of movement in the realities of their own bodies.

Kineticism and Luminism were the focus of two Northern European groups: the Nul group in Amsterdam, which included Herman de Vries (b. 1931), and the Zero group in Düsseldorf, formed by Heinz Mack (b. 1931) and Otto Piene (b. 1928), and joined later by Günther Uecker (b. 1930) whose panels, bristling

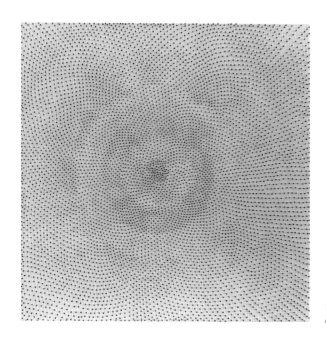

18 Günther Uecker
Kreis, Kreise 1970

with nails, trapped and scattered light in their undulations. The postwar Spatialism of the Italian Lucio Fontana (1899–1968), defined by him as an art of space and light, had affinities with this. By the 1960s it was influencing artists – Michelangelo Pistoletto (b. 1933), and Mario Merz (b. 1925) – who would later be associated with Arte Povera. Pistoletto in mid-decade, however, was making Pop-like collages of people on mirrored surfaces. It was thus impossible for viewers to look at these works – *Man Reading* (1967) and *Two People* (1962) for example – without themselves becoming associated with the figures depicted.

The concentration upon the commonplaces, even the banalities, of existence evident in Pop identify it as another flowering of realism in art. Hitherto used to describe art as diverse as the mid-nineteenth-century paintings of Courbet, Millet and Daumier, the Cubism of Picasso and Braque, and, within the tag 'Socialist Realism', the glorifying, propagandistic imagery of Stalinist Russia, realism again became useful as a catch-all term for what seemed a general move away from the abstraction and individual emotional expressiveness of early postwar art. In France, the work of Arman (b. 1928), Daniel Spoerri (b. 1930), Yves Klein, César, Niki de Saint-Phalle (b. 1930), Jean Tinguely and others was, in fact, called Nouveau Réalisme in

1960 by the critic Pierre Restany, in preference to the English label Pop. In part, this terminological difference can be seen as a tactic in a larger ideological battle. The touring exhibitions of US painting in the latter half of the preceding decade had done much to establish New York as the pre-eminent centre of modern art, an honour hitherto held throughout the modern period by Paris. Referring to things as Nouveau Réaliste, an umbrella category that would include Pop, was one way of assuring the world that little had changed with regard to the balance of cultural power.

A tongue-in-cheek instance of the power play was the full-page advertisement placed in the Swiss journal *Art International*, in the summer of 1964, by the New York art dealer Leo Castelli. That year saw not only the staging of the third Documenta, the quinquennial international survey of contemporary art held in Kassel, Germany, but also the Venice Biennale. Castelli's artists, Johns, Rauschenberg and others, were showing at both, as well as in Paris and London. The advertisement showed this as the map of a military advance, the artists pushing out from these four centres into the rest of Europe. Rauschenberg won the first prize at Venice that year, a success

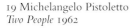

19 Michelangelo Pistoletto
Two People 1962

which was hailed by many as conclusive evidence if not of the general superiority of US art over European, then at least of the challenge which it was throwing down. Annette Michelson, a US critic then living in Paris, reviewed the Biennale for *Art International*. She described the reception given to the view of the exhibition put forward by Dr Alan Solomon, the American critic and historian, thus: 'in affirming the unquestioned superiority of contemporary American art over that of Europe, in treating this superiority as a matter of course and of common international understanding, [he] indicated that America's artists had not come to participate in a meeting of minds, a "cultural exchange," or to engage in competition with peers, but to collect an official prize and its attendant benefits. The howls of rage which greeted this statement were moderately touching, but no more.'

The term Nouveau Réalisme had been invented in 1960 apropos an exhibition in Milan which included the work of Tinguely, Arman and Klein as well as that of Raymond Hains (b. 1926) and Jacques de la Villeglé (b. 1926), two artists who worked in collages made from fragments of torn posters. Contrast the directness of Robert Indiana's response to signs, or that of Edward Ruscha or Tom Wesselman, with the self-consciously manipulative way in which Hains and de la Villeglé reproduced the effect of weathering and ageing on their materials. Another measure of the differences between the US and France can be seen in the comparison between the sculpture of César

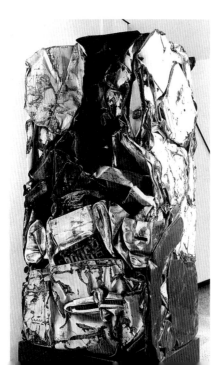

20 César
The Yellow Buick 1961

21 John Chamberlain
Miss Lucy Pink 1963

and John Chamberlain (b. 1927). Both were making art from old car bodies, but whereas César's automobile compressions of 1961–62 used the power imparted by the scrapyard's vehicle crusher to turn the car into its own tombstone, Chamberlain's *Coo Wha Zee* (1962) or *Miss Lucy Pink* (1963) appropriated the bent and folded panels because they were ideal material from which to make abstract sculpture. The metal was infinitely pliable, yet held its shape, and its surfaces were coloured in a way that hinted at, but did not quite resemble, painting.

Klein's notorious show, *Le Vide*, at Iris Clert's Paris gallery in 1958 had confronted visitors with an entirely empty space. Arman had responded two years later with *Le Plein*, emptying into the space the contents of several rubbish carts in a gesture that amplified his 'poubelles', glass cases filled with the contents of wastepaper baskets. In similar vein, Daniel Spoerri's 'Tableaux Pièges', such as *Le Fer à Repasser* (1960), presented the contents of a tabletop as a wall-mounted panel. Many of Arman's assemblages involved filling glass cases with identical or very similar objects: *Arteriosclerose* (1961), for example, is a collection of forks and spoons, while the case of *En Fer* (1961) houses a variety of gas burners. Arman's was a plenitude different from the serial order of repeated images in New York except, perhaps, in *Air Mail Stickers* (1962) by Yayoi Kusama (b. 1929), or Warhol's *trompe-l'oeil* painting of 'Glass – Handle With Care' labels. Others associated with Nouveau Réalisme included Martial Raysse (b. 1936), the Italian Mimmo Rotella (b. 1918), and

22

23

31

22 (left) Arman
Arteriosclerose 1961

23 (right) Yayoi Kusama
Air Mail Stickers 1962

Christo and Jeanne-Claude (both b. 1935), whose wrapped objects were descendants of the prototypical Surrealist work *The Enigma of Isidore Ducasse* (1920) by Man Ray (1890–1976).

Whereas Happenings in the US signal the extension of Abstract Expressionist gestures into the environment, there is an element of showmanship in Nouveau Réalisme which, although greatly influenced by Pollock's example, more significantly involves the actions of the artist in the final work. Klein's designation of a particular blue pigment as his own – International Klein Blue – and his subsequent employment of nude female models to smear it under his direction 24 onto prepared surfaces to make his *anthropométries* is only the most famous example. Arman's *colères* (tantrums) attempted to seize the instant in which an object, often an instrument, was violently destroyed, by fixing the resultant fragments in their precise relationships. Tinguely's motorized junk sculptures derived much from their spectacular effects. Niki de Saint-Phalle used a gun to fire paint at her canvases. Klein 'painted' with fire. All of these activities pushed the persona of the artist to the fore, putting a new shine on Duchamp's demonstration that it is the artist, purely because he or she *is* the artist, who has the power to designate something as art. The Italian Piero Manzoni (1933–63) who, like Klein, died young in the early 1960s, made a number of ironic gestures in this spirit. He signed a model, making her the artwork. Canning his own shit, he offered it for sale, priced according to how much its weight would be 25 worth in gold. Inflating a balloon he made *The Artist's Breath* (1961), a perishable reflection of Duchamp's glass vial, *50cc air de Paris* (1919).

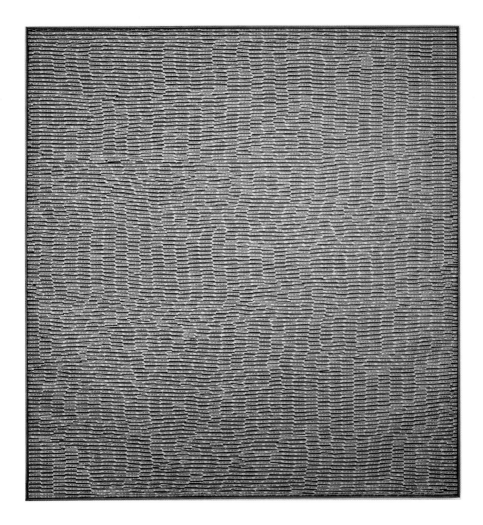

Matching the instantaneity of Arman's *colères*, the British artist
John Latham (b. 1921) began making 'one second drawings' by
applying the merest squeeze to a spray-gun trigger. These were seen
not as finished images, but as traces of a Minimal 'event'. Earlier,
having made images in the 1950s reminiscent of Klein's *anthropométries*, he had started to use books in sculptural constructions and
wall assemblages. Several of these assemblages had moveable parts and
could thus be displayed in a number of configurations. The books
stuck to the multi-panelled surface of *The Great Uncle Estate* (1960)

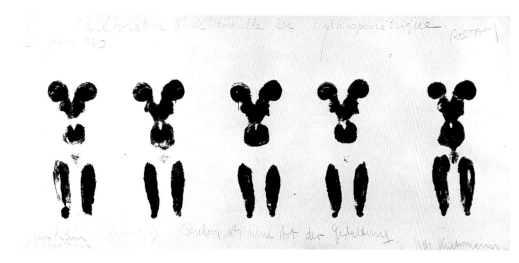

could each be held open by wires at pages painted either red, yellow or blue, thus allowing the work to exist in three different modes. This mobility of final form was also a factor in the 'variable paintings' of the Swede Öyvind Fahlström (1928–76). In these, a number of magnetized or hinged cartoon-like pieces could be moved around the surface to produce many different possible paintings. The options built into these game-like works, described by Fahlström as 'machinery to make paintings', enabled him to combine the chance nature of reality with his intentions as an artist.

If what went on behind the Iron Curtain, that postwar political reality made concrete by the Berlin Wall in 1961, was Socialist Realism, there were strong grounds for describing Pop as Capitalist Realism. This label was used in association with the exhibitions organized by René Block in his Berlin gallery in the mid-1960s. It had also been used in 1963 when Gerhard Richter (b. 1932) and Konrad Lueg (1939–96) – better known subsequently as the influential dealer Konrad Fischer – organized *A Demonstration for Capitalist Realism*, occupying a room tableau in a furniture store. Both Richter and Sigmar Polke (b. 1941), who participated in the *Demonstration*, were using media imagery as source material for their paintings. Clear superficial parallels exist between their work and US Pop. Warhol's preoccupation with glamour and the coverage of death and disaster in the tabloids is mirrored in Richter's works, such as 27 *Olympia* (1967), taken from an image in a Readers' Wives magazine, and his painting of the student nurse victims of a serial killer, *Eight*

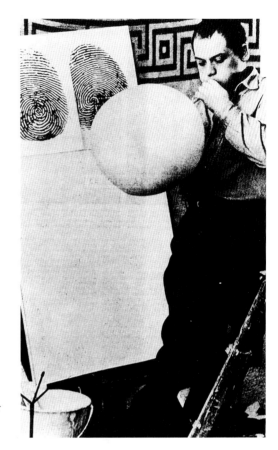

24 (left) Yves Klein
Celebration of a New Anthropometric Era
1960

25 (right) Piero Manzoni making
The Artist's Breath 1961

26 (below) Konrad Lueg and Gerhard Richter
A Demonstration for Capitalist Realism
11 October 1963

Student Nurses (1966). Polke, as Lichtenstein was producing cartoon-ized versions of Picasso, Monet and the Abstract Expressionist gesture, gave us *Moderne Kunst* (1968). This 'abstract composition' of splodges and doodles is painted with a white border and its title written along the bottom edge as if it were, in fact, not an abstract painting at all, but the faithful reproduction of the page of a book. This painting is both modern art and at the same time an invaluable guide to enable us to recognize modern art should we ever encounter it. Polke also used different fabrics as painting surfaces, making it hard to view his art in the rarefied isolation of the gallery without remembering and considering domestic reality.

Wolf Vostell (b. 1932), whose works were exhibited in René Block's 'Capitalist Realism' and 'Homage to Berlin' exhibitions, had been blurring pages from illustrated magazines since 1961. *Concrete*

27 (left) Gerhard Richter
Olympia 1967

28 (right) Sigmar Polke
Moderne Kunst 1968

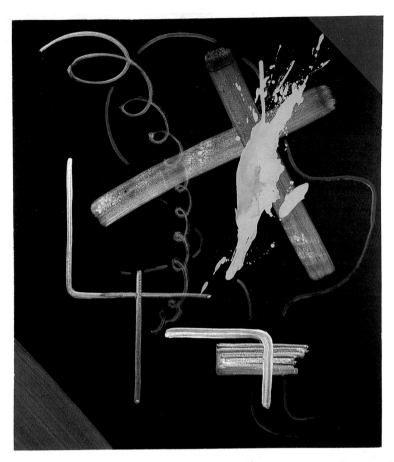

Moderne Kunst

Slabs (1961) makes direct reference to Germany's politically divided state and to the Berlin Wall which was erected in that year. Vostell became involved the following year with Fluxus. As its name implies, this was a loose association of more or less like-minded artists rather than a well-defined group. It shared a Dadaist sensibility with US Happenings, particularly to the ideas of the American composer John Cage (1912–92), and worked across the boundaries between art, music and literature. A close relationship also existed with the contemporary Situationist movement, which, through the engineering of events looked for *détournement*, the turning of social conditions

37

29 Wolf Vostell *Berlin–Fieber V* 1973

against themselves to reveal their true character. Situationism had a strong political figurehead in Guy Debord, but art practice featured largely in its original manifestos through the neo-Dada input of the Danish painter Asger Jorn (1914–73). Vostell's Fluxus 'actions', and those of Joseph Beuys (1921–86) whom he met in 1963, very often had explicit political content. Later, Vostell would want to contribute to a Documenta by placing a US F-111, abiding symbol of the political realities of his divided country, on the roof of the main exhibition building in Kassel, a project that remained unfulfilled. His actions remained simple in conception and forthright in intent: 'I want to find out whether rules for types of behaviour in daily life can be obtained from actions with a model character, whether impulses emanating from me can be applied in everyday life to counter intolerance, stupidity and oppression.'

Although there were many points of connection with US Pop, the more overt political tone of this German art and the even more explicitly stated ironies of Polke and Richter were felt to constitute a significant difference. Contrasting Vostell's work with the multiple images silk-screened onto Rauschenberg's canvases of the mid-1960s, the German artist K. P. Brehmer (b. 1938) said: 'For Rauschenberg, for example, Kennedy is just a smear of colour. For Vostell, Kennedy is something different – he is a politician, he stands in a political environment and this has a completely different significance.'

38

In Britain, the 1960s idea of Pop, feeding through from the activities and theoretical discussions of the Independent Group in the 1950s, was largely celebrated as an aspect of the style revolution. There were exceptions, such as the paintings and collages of Colin Self (b. 1941) which commented in a more forthright manner on the politics of the Cold War and the threat of nuclear catastrophe. Richard Hamilton, too, continued to dissect domestic politics. *Swingeing London* (1968), for example, was derived from a press photo of Mick Jagger and the art dealer Robert Fraser being arrested on a drugs charge, and questioned whether there had really been a liberalizing of attitude during the period. It would be wrong, though, to think of US Pop as being altogether unconcerned with the political dimension of the reality it portrayed. Ed Kienholz's tableaux placed the seedier aspects of life – prostitution, abortion and destitution – centre stage; Oldenburg's humour was not without its acerbic edge: a drawing for a public monument in London proposes a giant ballcock on the Thames near the Houses of Parliament, sinking and rising with the tide; and in spite of Warhol's increasing disinclination to speak about any message his work might have, the combination of monochrome panel and images in a work like *Silver Disaster: Electric Chair* (1963) provides social comment in addition to acknowledging the continuing development of abstract painting.

30 Andy Warhol *Silver Disaster: Electric Chair* 1963

In his 'Unfurled' series of 1960–61, Morris Louis (1912–62) ran paint in rough diagonals off the outer edges of unstretched canvases. Cropping and stretching produced paintings, as with *Beta Upsilon* (1960) or *Omicron* (1961), for example, which had a large, central empty V flanked by variously coloured ribbons anchoring the sides to the bottom edge. Influenced by the 'drawing' inherent in Jackson Pollock's skeins of dribbled paint and the integrated flatness of paintings made by staining unprimed canvas of Helen Frankenthaler (b. 1928), Louis had arrived at a way of producing thoroughly flat paintings whose form, derived through the channelling of paint under the influence of gravity rather than purposive application of a loaded brush, served as a bracing structure for an absent image. At around the same time, Kenneth Noland (b. 1924) was executing 'targets', including *Song* (1958), *Breath* (1959) and *Split Spectrum* (1961), which comprised concentric circles of variously coloured paints. Like Louis' 'Unfurleds', these were on unprimed canvas to emphasize their flatness. The absence of conspicuous brushwork in these paintings, together with the bright and direct colours of the new acrylic paint they used, differed from the gestural tonality of Abstract Expressionism. The style, consequently, was referred to as Hard-edge painting, or Post-painterly Abstraction.

31 Morris Louis *Omicron* 1961

32 Kenneth Noland
Song 1958

Critical opinion of these painters in the first half of the 1960s clearly shows that a battle was taking place. Clement Greenberg, the most influential writer on art in the quarter-century after the war, spoke of them as successors to the great flowering of US artistic talent that was Abstract Expressionism. In his writings since before the Second World War, Greenberg had put forward a particularly persuasive account of the history of modern art. According to this, the succession of steps from Impressionism, through Cubism, Matisse and Mondrian, up to Abstract Expressionism could be seen as an internal development of the means and possibilities of painting itself. What could be understood to be taking place in modernism was, for Greenberg, a critical and reflective realization of painting's essential qualities. Painting could be distinguished from other art forms by the rectangle of the canvas and its two-dimensionality. Before the war, in common with many prominent US intellectuals, Greenberg had espoused a quasi-Marxist ideology, but his views, like those of so many others, were profoundly affected by the Holocaust and Stalinism, the latter widely embraced during the war but afterwards perceived as a threat. Subsequently, despite Greenberg's denial that it was good in itself, abstraction became, within his criticism, the provider of a guaranteed realm of aesthetic quality removed from what was now a fatally compromised reality. In this light, the thoroughly flat abstraction of Louis and Noland appeared akin to modernism's ultimate self-realization.

The immediate question that such an analysis raises is, What happens now? If painting has achieved a realization of its essential qualities, what is there left for it to do? One solution was for painting to extend itself into the third dimension, something that had hitherto been the exclusive property of sculptural form. Works such as *Watusi* (1965) by Sven Lukin (b. 1934) and *Tailspan* (1965) by the Englishman Richard Smith, who had gone to New York after attending London's Royal College of Art, laid canvas over stretchers that jutted out from the wall. Lee Bontecou (b. 1931) kept painting's rectangular frame, but constructed within it untitled contoured surfaces of sheet metal and wire. The painted structures of Anne Truitt (b. 1921), such as *Late Snow* (1964), were free-standing, while those of Jo Baer (b. 1929), in which the visual 'incident' was kept entirely around the deep edges of an otherwise white canvas, remained on the wall although they were not necessarily hung at the standard height. The canvases of Ellsworth Kelly (b. 1923) were divided into a small number of clearly defined areas of flat colour: *Orange/Green* (1966), *Green/White* (1967), and so on. Sometimes the areas of colour would coincide with the shape of the canvas, a logical alternative given Kelly's parallel production of simply-shaped, painted sheet metal sculptures. Rather than moving into an area of production that was neither quite painting nor sculpture, Kelly continued along the lines of Picasso, David Smith (1906–65) and even Barnett Newman, all of whom did both. One of Greenberg's own preferred champions of the continuing strength of modern art was the English sculptor Anthony Caro (b. 1924). Caro, himself making figurative bronzes, had worked in the studio of Henry Moore (1898–1986) for a time in the 1950s, following which he had visited the US. There he met Kenneth Noland, among others, and David Smith, a painter as well as a sculptor, who used metal in a way which was, if not exactly representational, at least pictorial. After war-time experience in an engine works Smith was not accustomed to casting the fine art material of bronze, but rather to welding the I-beams and plate of industrial steel. In the US, Mark di Suvero (b. 1933) and Charles Ginnever (b. 1931) were also working in this way, the moveable parts of di Suvero's large pieces drawing something, too, from the mobiles of Alexander Calder (1898–1976). The trip was liberating for Caro. He wrote: 'There is a fine art quality about European art, even when it's made from junk. America made me see that there are no barriers and no regulations.'

On his return to Britain, Caro began to weld, using plates, beams,

33 Ellsworth Kelly
Orange and Green 1966

rods and tubes of steel and aluminium with which to construct his sculptures. These new works were strikingly abstract compositions, the various parts setting up relationships within the overall shape of each piece, a shape emphasized by Caro's habit of painting the finished sculpture a single colour. Nevertheless, the red *Early One Morning* (1962), in whose profile lingers the ghost of Moore's reclining nudes, and the yellow, expansively horizontal *Prairie* (1967) are only two examples showing that figuration had been not simply rejected, but transmuted into allusive reference. Alongside Caro, a number of others, notably Phillip King (b. 1934), Tim Scott (b. 1937) and Michael Bolus (b. 1934), made up a 'New Generation' of British sculptors anxious to avail itself of the new freedom to use a greatly expanded range of materials. Scott's *For 'Cello* (1965) and

35

King's *Genghis Khan* (1963), for instance, both used plastic and fibre-glass. Of them all, though, it was Caro who offered an escape to all those keen to see a continuation of the modernist tradition. After Louis and Noland, his colourful sculptures seemed a way forward, one in tune with the abstract formalism of Ellsworth Kelly, the busier canvases of Larry Zox (b. 1936), the sprayed paintings of Jules Olitski (b. 1922) and the choreographed elliptical dots of Larry Poons (b. 1937). Another noteworthy feature of Caro's sculpture, one shared with the Minimal art contemporary with it, was that it stood directly on the floor. Thus it occupied the same space as those who viewed it rather than a separate, aesthetic realm.

Minimalism then, a movement most usually identified with sculptural endeavour, can be understood, in part at least, as a continuation of painting by other means. Like many of the other names of movements in the history of modern art – Impressionism, Fauvism, Cubism – the label 'Minimalist' was applied by critics to the work of Donald Judd (1928–94), Robert Morris (b. 1931), Dan Flavin (1933–96) and Carl Andre in 1965 with pejorative intent. Other artists – Ronald Bladen (1918–88), Robert Grosvenor (b. 1937), Larry Bell (b. 1939), Bill Bollinger (b. 1939), Stephen Antonakos (b. 1926), Judy Chicago (born Judy Gerowitz in 1939), Tony DeLap (b. 1927) among them – were making work that could be viewed, more or less, within what was understood by the term Minimalism. However, just as a discussion of Cubism turns mainly upon the contributions of Picasso and Braque, the key features of Minimalism are most easily recognizable in the art of Judd, Morris, Flavin and

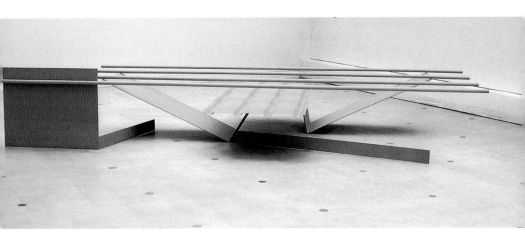

Andre. Sol LeWitt (b. 1928) and Robert Smithson (1928–73) were both also associated with the tendency, but their main significance lies elsewhere and will be discussed later.

The critic Barbara Rose offered Duchamp's designation of an object as 'readymade' and the decision of the Russian painter Kasimir Malevich (1878–1935) to exhibit a single black square on a white background as the historical poles of Minimalism. 'It is important to keep in mind', she wrote, 'that both Duchamp's and Malevich's decisions were renunciations – on Duchamp's part, of the notion of the uniqueness of the art object and its differentiation from common objects, and on Malevich's part, a renunciation of the notion that art must be complex.' Judd, who began as a painter, wrote in his 1965

34 (left) Richard Smith
Tailspan 1965

35 (above) Anthony Caro
Prairie 1967

36 (right) Phillip King
Genghis Khan 1963

37 Robert Morris *Untitled (Slab)* 1968

essay, 'Specific Objects', that much art then being made could no longer be described as either painting or sculpture. He termed it, instead, 'three-dimensional work'. This was also remarked upon by Clement Greenberg: 'What seems definite is that [artists] commit themselves to the third dimension because it is, among other things, a co-ordinate that art has to share with non-art (as Dada, Duchamp and others already saw).'

There were other terms around at the time, most notably ABC art and Primary Structures (the title of an exhibition at New York's Jewish Museum in 1966), but Minimalism is the one that has persisted. The richly gestural paintings of the preceding generation of artists, the Abstract Expressionists, seemed replete with emotional and expressive content. In contrast, this new work looked mono-chromatic, engineered, impersonal, and by analogy, if a Jackson Pollock or a work by Willem de Kooning (b. 1904) was 'full' of art, then the blankness of Morris's low, rectangular plywood *Untitled (Slab)* (1968), the egregious simplicity of Andre's floor-hugging arrangements of house bricks, or the obduracy of Donald Judd's untitled box-like wooden constructions predominantly painted in his favourite cadmium red light, must have seemed pretty 'empty'. In what is taken as the first use of the term, the philosopher Richard Wollheim wrote in 1965 that the emptiness of these works 'might be expressed by saying that they have a minimal art content: in that either they are to an extreme degree undifferentiated in themselves and therefore possess very low content of any kind, or else the differentiation that they do exhibit, which may in some cases be very considerable, comes not from the artist but from a nonartistic source, like nature or the factory'.

46

38 Donald Judd *Untitled* 1965

For Judd, the blank look of this art was symptomatic of what he saw as the growing irrelevance of traditional aesthetic attitudes. His work was simple and formally pared down because of a wish not to employ compositional effects. Composition emphasizes internal relationships between the various parts of a work and in so doing plays down the impact of the work as a whole. Judd's desire was that the viewer should concentrate, for example, on the upper horizontal bar and the units fixed at regular intervals along its lower edge of *Untitled* (1965) as a single, whole 'thing'. In this he is close to the American composer John Cage who, having met and studied under Arnold Schoenberg (1874–1951), rejected his example because of a wish to produce music that was not composed. This idea can be seen, too, in the paintings being made by Frank Stella (b. 1936) as the 1960s began.

In 1958, Stella made a series of black paintings, the rectilinear pattern of whose striped surfaces was closely related to the shape of the canvas. *Getty's Tomb, II* (1959), for example, has a band running up one edge, across the top and down the other edge of the canvas, 40 while the remainder of the surface is filled with concentric bands executed in the same way. These works are striking for the interdependence that exists between them as objects – stretched canvases of certain dimensions – and the images they carry on their surfaces. They are, in Judd's terms, 'one thing'. Once decisions have been made as to the dimensions of the stretcher and the organizational logic of the marks, it remains for the painting to be executed, rather than built up, through the balancing of one brush stroke against another. There is a distinct order to these paintings; they are regular and structured. It is an order, as Judd said, that 'is not rationalistic

47

and underlying but is simply order, like that of continuity, one thing after another'. Following the black paintings Stella made some further series using aluminium and then copper paint, each developing the idea of a congruence between painting as object and painting as image. For these series he began to experiment with shaped canvases, cutting notches out of the standard rectangle for the aluminium paintings, and constructing surfaces in a variety of rectilinear shapes for the copper paintings.

48

39 Barnett Newman *Who's Afraid of Red, Yellow and Blue III* 1966–67

Asked by the critic Bruce Glaser why he wanted to avoid compositional effects, Judd replied: 'Well, those effects tend to carry with them all the structure, values, feelings of the whole European tradition. It suits me fine if that's all down the drain. ...The qualities of European art so far [are] innumerable and complex, but the main way of saying it is that they're linked up with a philosophy – rationalism.' This perhaps sounds intemperate and dismissive, but it is more important to recognize the positive aspect of Judd's thought

49

at this time. European rationalism was 'pretty much discredited as a way of finding out what the world's like' because the world was now a place of different character. The repetitions of daily life, the proliferation of consumer goods, and all those other things remarked and reflected on in Pop, were forcing a reconsideration of how the passing of time, the making of things and the understanding of an object's uniqueness were to be valued. Judd wrote elsewhere, 'The objections to painting and sculpture are going to sound more intolerant than they are. They are qualifications. The disinterest in painting and sculpture is a disinterest in doing it again, not in it as it is being done by those who developed the last advanced versions.'

The last advanced versions, for him, were the paintings of Stella, Noland, Louis and, from an older generation, Barnett Newman. The latter's mature style, dating back to his 1948 *Onement I*, a single stripe running vertically down the centre of an otherwise monochrome surface, made it hard to view his paintings in the conventional terms of a relationship between figure and ground. Because his stripes, or 'zips', always reached the top and bottom edges of his canvases, they served to define and articulate the proportions of a flat surface as much as, if not more than, they appeared to populate a potentially deep colour space. Insofar as they were spatial, this had more to do with the manner in which their large size physically overwhelmed the spectator. For example, the large red expanses of *Vir Heroicus Sublimis* (1951), or *Who's Afraid of Red, Yellow and Blue III* (1966–67), both paintings of nearly twenty feet in length, are almost impossible to absorb in their entirety, and thus provide something like an environment of colour that encloses the viewer. This environmental quality was something that would become increasingly important as the 1960s progressed.

Acknowledging the significance of the uneasiness with rationalism, Barbara Rose saw a common root for Pop and Minimalism in the US tradition of pragmatism. Not only the philosophies of William James and John Dewey, but also the Precisionists of the early years of the century were identified as parts of an indigenous tradition. A search for heroism in the industrial landscape or the domestic interiors of the country, evident in the painting and photography of Charles Sheeler (1883–1965) and Charles Demuth (1883–1935) connected with the depersonalized and factory-like methods of Warhol and Judd's insistence upon making art which eschewed illusionism. It is in making considerations of this sort that the spiritual side of Minimal art starts to become apparent. Rose quotes

39

40 Frank Stella *Getty's Tomb, II* 1959

Robert Henri (1865–1929), a key figure in the Ashcan school of US realists at the turn of the century, admiring machine tools for the directness with which they fulfil the function for which they were conceived: 'There is no "Art" about them, they have not been *made* beautiful, they *are* beautiful.' Similarly, the directness of Shaker design was to influence Sheeler, and its unornamented style was to appear as a precursor to Judd's rigorous approach, particularly as he moved into furniture design and architecture. Later in his career, Judd moved to Marfa, Texas, renovating and altering several buildings in and around 41 the town as optimum environments in which to display his own art and that of his contemporaries which he had collected over the

41 Donald Judd's permanent installation of works, East Building, La Mansana de Chinati, Marfa, Texas

42 Donald Judd *Untitled* 1968

43 Frank Stella *Delaware Crossing* from 'Benjamin Moore' series 1961

years. The over-arching nature of this project lends weight to Rose's view. She wrote: 'Judd's rejection of illusionism is deeply rooted in the pragmatic tenet that truth to facts is an ethical value. For Judd, illusionism is close to immorality, because it falsifies reality. The pragmatist demands an absolute correspondence between facts and reality; things must be as they appear to be. Any disjunction between appearance and reality, such as illusionism, which distorts the facts, is sharply felt as an affront to truth, because pragmatism equates truth with the physical facts as experienced.'

Minimal art, then, did not represent anything or refer directly to anything else in such a way as to render its own authenticity dependent upon the adequacy of its illustrative likeness to that other thing. It was not metaphorical and it did not offer itself as the symbol of some spiritual or metaphysical truth. This fact also accounts for the vast number of works of art called 'Untitled', since giving something a name would render it subordinate to whatever it was named after. In the same interview with Bruce Glaser quoted above, Frank Stella said of his paintings, 'What you see is what you see.' He quoted his friend Hollis Frampton (1936–84), the photographer and film-maker, in stating that his aim was to produce a painting that allowed the paint to look 'as good as it did in the can'. A kind of literalization of this desire can be seen in Stella's 1961 'Benjamin Moore' series. Six different linear patterns were painted in each of the three primary and three secondary colours – red, yellow, blue, green, orange, purple – using colours available in the Benjamin Moore range of household paints.

43

The non-composed, non-referential abstractness of Minimalism offered considerable resistance to the standard methods of art appreciation, but there were other factors behind its oblique muteness. One was concerned with how its objects were made. For example, Judd's early sculptures were made in wood, but this material soon gave way to metal and perspex. Iron, steel, copper and aluminium had greater strength at smaller thicknesses and could be engineered much more exactly to the required dimensions. In addition, their surfaces could take or present colour in very different ways to wood, and in the case of, for example, the amber perspex used in *Untitled* (1968) the colour was literally *in* the material, not applied to its surface at all.

42

In Dan Flavin's case, the colour he used was not 'applied' to anything at all. Flavin first used electric light in his constructions in 1961, moving to fluorescent tubes two years later with *The Diagonal of May 25, 1963*. Placing them initially on the wall in different alignments and combinations, he soon began devising arrangements for specific places. There are several challenges to the *status quo* in these works. Flavin's purchase of standard neon tubes and fitments meant that the evidence of his individual touch on his materials was never going to be an issue. This 'absence' of the artist is corroborated in the decision of Judd, LeWitt and others to have their works fabricated by others according to a set of specifications supplied by the artist. The work may well be unique (though only because the instructions had been carried out once), yet the person or people who physically made it are not necessarily the artists.

The physical presence of the neon tubes and their holders is always significant, but, more than anything, Flavin's material is the coloured light they emit. Newman's 'zips' are suggested in the vertical arrangement of the tubes in *The Nominal Three (To William of*

44 Dan Flavin *The Nominal Three (To William of Ockham)* 1963

Ockham) (1963), and the title implies that Flavin has used the philosopher's famous razor, 'Entities are not to be multiplied without necessity', to reduce the problems of art-making to the fundamentals of pure, disembodied colour. Several of the works of the mid-1960s have the generic title *Monument for V. Tatlin*, and in 1966 he made the first of his installations set at an angle across the corner of a room. The effect of this is to remodel the space by making the corner 'disappear'. The artist Mel Bochner (b. 1940) wrote of Flavin exhibiting an 'acute awareness of the phenomenology of rooms. ...[His] demolished corners convert the simple facts of roomness into operative factors.'

As mentioned earlier, although it differed in many other ways from Caro's composed sculptures, Minimalism shared with them a rejection of the plinth. The plinth, like the frame of a painting, isolates a

45 Carl Andre *Equivalents I–VIII* 1966

sculpture, removing it, as it were, to a discrete aesthetic space where
it may be contemplated. Art on the floor had to be viewed not as
something apart, but as one more thing in the viewer's physical
space. Carl Andre's work in brick, wood and metal plate continually
emphasized its relationship with the floor on which it was placed.
(An early job as a freight guard on the US railways offering him
endless views across the plains to the horizon is often adduced as the
inspiration behind this preoccupation with horizontality.) Andre's
sculptures, made from small units placed together in simple, regular
arrangements, are a classic example of the non-rational order Judd
referred to as 'one thing after another'. The 137 bricks in *Lever*
(1966), placed in a single line along the floor, exhibit the pulse of
repetition that Judd and, of course, a Pop artist like Warhol were
anxious to deal with. When Warhol was asked, 'Why did you start
painting soup cans?', he replied, 'Because I used to drink it. I used to
have the same lunch every day, for twenty years, I guess, the same
thing over and over again.' The extended modularity also recalls, in a
different orientation, Constantin Brancusi's 'Endless Columns', the
first of which was made in 1920. This work Andre had previously
acknowledged in the double pyramid of his 1959 *Cedar Piece*.

In the early 1960s, Andre made a group of works using large blocks of expanded polystyrene. Although not permanently fixed together in any way, they were interleaved so as to form simple joints. Eschewing even this level of complexity, he subsequently opted for a straightforward placement of one element next to another. Wanting his sculpture to be 'low' and ground-hugging, he decided, on a 1965 canoeing trip in New England, that it needed to be as flat as water. Andre's New York exhibition of the following year realized this aim in his showing of *Equivalents I–VIII*, eight sculptures each made from 120 bricks. Comprising two layers of 60 bricks, their shapes were determined by four of the possible factorial

46 Carl Andre *37 Pieces of Work* 1969

combinations of the number, each combination leading to two shapes depending upon the orientation of the bricks. The eight were therefore equivalent numerically and volumetrically. In the years following, Andre's works would get lower still, using square plates of a variety of metals arranged in simple configurations on the floor, sometimes to spectacular effect as with *37 Pieces of Work* (1969) which brought 36 separate works together to make a 37th in the atrium of the Guggenheim Museum. In order that they be experienced in full, the spectator was invited to walk on these 'plains'. The literal feel of the work, the particular density of the metal, its sound and its resistance to the tread are all part of what it can give to the 'spectator'. Yet again Duchamp is called to mind for his strictures against a visual art that was purely 'retinal'.

An art that saw itself as new in some way suggested that it should also be judged as good or bad according to new standards. Greenberg had asked that art might demonstrate 'quality', and his argument for this derived from Kant's aesthetic theory. In place of quality, however, and in defiance of the rationalist tradition within which Kant figures prominently, Judd asserted that 'a work of art need only be interesting'. The media theorist Marshall McLuhan had already noted that television promotes interest as the key quality in the viewing experience. More than the particular subject matter of a programme, it is the manner in which the camera gets close to and penetrates its subject that draws us in. Not only should art resemble ordinary things, but the way in which the spectator views it should be grounded in an everyday experience. Of all the artists associated with Minimalism, it was Robert Morris who did most to describe this aspect of the style. Starting in 1966, he published a series of articles in which the creation and viewing of sculpture were analysed in depth. In particular, he elaborated the understanding of Minimalism in relation to phenomenology. The French philosopher Maurice Merleau-Ponty had published his study *The Phenomenology of Perception* in 1961, and there are many parallels between the nature and experience of Minimal art and the way in which Merleau-Ponty characterizes the reciprocal nature of the process whereby individuals come to an awareness of the space and objects around them: 'Space is not the setting (real or logical) in which things are arranged, but the means whereby the position of things becomes possible.'

In a way which seems akin to Judd's stress on the work of art as 'one thing', 'a whole thing', Morris, in 'Notes on Sculpture', proposes a work of sculpture as a gestalt object. That is, a simple form

46

whose total shape can be immediately apprehended by the viewer. A consequence of such simplicity of form is that, once recognized, 'all the information about it, *qua* gestalt, is exhausted'. This then frees one to consider other aspects, of scale, proportion, material, surface, for instance, in cohesive relation to this fundamental unity. Given the undifferentiated character of this type of work, the onlooker becomes aware of the viewing process as having duration. Whereas looking into a painting had allowed one to lose oneself in the world it offered, an exploration that was often described as timeless, or as occurring outside time, this was quite clearly not the case when one was confronted with Morris's *Untitled* (1965): four, waist-high mirrored cubes. Walking around and between the separate parts of this sculpture allows one to experience the gallery space and one's own and others' bodies as a fractured and disjunctive reality. His earlier exhibition, in 1963, at the Green Gallery, New York, similarly articulated the space with a number of plain, quasi-architectural rectilinear forms.

In contrast to the positive tone of Morris's 'Notes' and Judd's 'Specific Objects', the critic Michael Fried's position was to resist the artistic claims of Minimalism. Fried had been a pupil of Greenberg and to a certain extent continued in his critical tradition. His uneasiness in the face of Minimal art was due largely to its rejection of

47 Robert Morris *Untitled* 1965

composition. You could not go 'into' these works in the same kind of way because there were no internal parts whose relationships could be pondered. This, rather than their literal boxy emptiness, is what Fried was referring to when he criticized Minimal sculpture, particularly the work of Judd and Morris, for being 'hollow'. They are devoid not of palpable stuff, but of the wherewithal to discern meaning. No longer can one ask, 'What is this about?' and expect the object in front of one to offer up an answer. What it can provide instead is a set of cues by which one can orient the experience of being in the gallery with it. This shift of the location of meaning out of the object and into its surrounding environment, was characterized by Fried in negative terms as a falling away from what art really was. 'Art', he said in his 1967 essay 'Art and Objecthood', 'degenerates as it approaches the condition of theatre.' Modernist art, which is to say the historical procession of images and objects produced within the social, industrial, economic and political conditions defined by the Industrial Revolution, sought authenticity in the rigour with which a medium explored its own techniques and materials. Minimal art, which Fried called 'literal' art, did not display this self-sufficiency. It existed *for* an audience (as Pop art did according to another influential American critic, Thomas Hess): it was something not quite life and not quite art, but rather the one somewhat self-consciously presenting itself as the other; an engineered 'situation' that occasioned reflection upon the qualities of the moment. Any meaning this kind of art had, then, was dependent upon the experience of the person viewing it. Such meaning was contingent, an aspect of the flux of everyday life.

Fried's notion of theatricality was not to be confused with drama, itself an art form that, along with music and dance, was now degenerating in a manner similar to art. The result was that, like the boundaries that were being blurred within art, those between the different art forms were, if not disappearing altogether, at least becoming thoroughly penetrable. Thus, Morris collaborated with the dancer Yvonne Rainer and as late as 1969 was describing himself in exhibition catalogues as a dancer; the composer Philip Glass (b. 1937) found the art world a more sympathetic context for his systems-based and unconventionally instrumented music than the concert hall; the taped speech of Steve Reich (b. 1936), looped and repeated as a means to introduce not only semantic content but also pitch and rhythm, paralleled art's pragmatic focus. Art now existed, in Morris's words, in a 'complex and expanded field'.

CHAPTER TWO

The Expanded Field

By the time Fried wrote about the dangers of art's degeneration towards theatre in 1967, the process was well under way. Fried's target was Minimalism, but Thomas Hess had made similar remarks about Pop in 1963. He wrote: 'The presence of a big audience is essential to complete a theatrical transformation. It is impossible to conceive of a Pop painting being produced until some plans are laid for its exhibition. Without its public reaction, the art object remains a fragment.' The consequence of the loosening of categories and the dismantling of interdisciplinary boundaries was a decade, from the mid-1960s to the mid-1970s, in which art took a great many different forms and names: Conceptual, Arte Povera, Process, Anti-Form, Land, Environmental, Body, Performance, and Political. These and others had their roots in Minimalism and the various offshoots of Pop and new realism. During this period there was also an increasing ease of access to and use of communication technologies: not only photography and film, but also sound, with the introduction of the audio cassette and the wider availability of recording equipment, and video, following the appearance on the market of the first standard non-broadcast machines.

When the US critic Lucy Lippard tried to document these developments in the mid-1970s her solution was to make what was in effect a scrapbook of articles, interviews and statements. There was no simple way in which all these tendencies could be disentangled from one another and examined separately. Likewise, the major survey exhibitions of the time, notably 'Live in Your Head: When Attitudes Become Form' (Kunsthalle, Berne and ICA, London, 1969), 'Software' (Jewish Museum, New York, 1970), 'Information' (MOMA, New York, 1970), and Documenta V organized by the Swiss curator Harald Szeeman in 1972, included most of these tendencies. Both the titles of those shows and the name of Lippard's book, *Six Years: The Dematerialisation of the Art Object from 1966 to 1972*, also spoke of the difficulty of grasping just what, during this period, art was becoming. Did the artwork have substantial form

48 Richard Serra
One Ton Prop (House of Cards) 1968–69

or was it a set of ideas on how to perceive the world? Was it a single object or was it more diffuse, occupying a much larger space? Was art to be found inside or outside the gallery? Art's changing face was neither the inexorable, nor indeed the inevitable forward march that the modernist notion of the avant-garde would understand. There was no preferred way of working that would cover all circumstances and requirements, and the idea that an artist should have a signature style, as Newman had his zips and Mark Rothko (1903–70) his fuzzy rectangles (the former also died in 1970), ceased to make much sense.

After Minimalism came post-Minimalism. That, at least, is the phrase the critic Robert Pincus-Witten coined to describe what followed. An alternative term was Process art, because in its final form, the materials and stages of manipulation that had been required in achieving it were made explicit. At other times it was dubbed Anti-Form. Taken together the names indicate what was beginning to appear by 1968 or so: an art that chronologically succeeded Minimalism which seized the freedoms it had brought and yet reacted against its formal rigidity.

49 Eva Hesse
Hang Up 1966

One Ton Prop (House of Cards) (1968–69) by Richard Serra (b. 1939) is simple and approximates a cube, but the four large, extremely heavy square metal plates of which it consists are only balanced against one another, not welded or otherwise rigidly fastened together; *One Ton Plate Prop* (1969) holds a plate upright and away from the wall by means of a lead cylinder equally precariously. But as well as this kind of play, in which the certainties, revelations and reassurances of art are shown as the potentially dangerous illusions they are, Serra was, from the outset, also concerned with the particular qualities of the environment in which his work was shown. Later this would result in a series of large-scale works for public places, but to begin with he dealt with the enclosed space of the gallery. *Casting* (1969) involved hurling molten lead into the angle between the floor and the wall of the gallery. The resultant, hardened moulds were then eased from the surfaces, turned, and displayed as a certain kind of evidence, both of the particular characteristics of the viewing space and of the process by which the work had been achieved.

A number of the sculptures of Eva Hesse (1936–70) also made use

63

of the various planes of the gallery. Like Serra, the geometric forms and repeated units of Minimalism make an appearance in her work, but not at all in the distanced, engineered way characteristic of that tendency. With one of her first major works, *Hang Up* (1966), Hesse made explicit the shift towards establishing an equivalence between the space of art and the space of its viewing. The piece is a large rectangular frame, thickly wrapped in bandage and painted in evenly graded shades of grey. Looping out from this frame to touch the floor some feet in front of it is a length of pliable metal rod. She wrote: 'It is extreme and that is why I like it and I don't like it. It's so absurd to have that long thin metal rod coming out of that structure. And it comes out a lot, about ten or eleven feet, and what is it coming out of? It is coming out of this frame – something and yet nothing and – oh! more absurdity – it is very, very finely done. The colours on the frame are very carefully graduated from light to dark – the whole thing is ludicrous.' This is as far from a Minimalist

49

50 (below) Eva Hesse *Accretion* 1968

51 (right) John McCracken *There's No Reason Not To* 1967

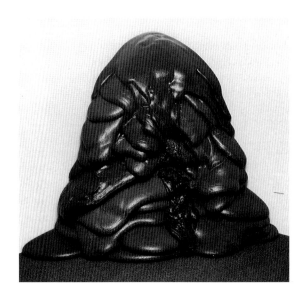

52 Lynda Benglis
For Carl Andre 1970

reliance on fabrication as a means to avoid 'craft' in art as it is possible to go.

50 The nonchalant pose adopted by the many handmade fibreglass tubes of Hesse's *Accretion* (1968) is reminiscent of the highly finished plank-like sculptures of John McCracken (b. 1934), such as his ten-
51 foot-high *There's No Reason Not To* (1967), but the individual glitches and modulations in the units perhaps point more towards the anchoring structure of the edge-to-bottom dribbles in Morris Louis's 'Unfurled' paintings. The sculptures of Lynda Benglis (b. 1941)

53 Bruce Nauman
Composite Photo of Two Messes on the Studio Floor (1967)

certainly have this pedigree. Pooling pigmented polyurethane produced works such as *Bullitt* (1969). Subsequently, as with *For Carl Andre* (1970), successive layers of variously coloured polyurethane foam were poured on top of one another.

'Anti-Form' was the title given to a short essay by Robert Morris in 1968. Looking back to the paintings of Morris Louis and, before him, Jackson Pollock, Morris promotes an art which takes process and 'holds on to it as part of the end form of the work'. The American artists Alan Saret (b. 1944), Keith Sonnier (b. 1941), Barry Le Va (b. 1941) and Morris himself were all at this time producing work which, instead of taking the form of distinctly bounded, discrete objects, involved the deployment of various materials over a large area.

Morris had followed his Minimalist pieces with large piles of felt strips, arrangements which could not possibly be replicated if the piece were to be shown subsequently in a different venue. In 1969 he selected an exhibition, 'Nine at Castelli', which included Hesse, Saret, Serra, Sonnier as well as Bruce Nauman (b. 1941), Bill Bollinger and Stephen Kaltenbach (b. 1940) as well as the Italian Arte Povera artists Giovanni Anselmo (b. 1934) and Gilberto Zorio (b. 1944). This show had considerable impact and made a strong case for the importance of process over product. In some respects the work it contained resembled a kind of dematerialization, an art made of the leftovers from some prior activity. Such appearances led the critic Max Kozloff to refer to it in his review as 'leavings'. This was literally the case with Nauman's *Composite Photo of Two Messes on the*

Studio Floor (1967), a collaged photo-documentation of the splashes, spillages and general detritus remaining after the completion of another work.

There had also been a show the previous year at John Gibson's gallery in New York, actually titled 'Anti-Form', which included some of those who would take part in the Castelli show as well as the Americans Robert Ryman (b. 1930) and Richard Tuttle (b. 1941) and the Belgian Panamarenko (b. 1940). During the previous decade Ryman had restricted himself to the use of white paint alone. Narrowing his palette in this way allowed for greater control in experimenting with other elements of a painting: its surface, scale, whether it was framed, how it was fastened to the wall, and so on. Panamarenko's plans and construction of idiosyncratic flying machines – his 1967 *Cockpit* was made from, among other things, a tin can and cellophane – are close in spirit to the interest of the British sculptor Barry Flanagan (b. 1941) in 'Pataphysics, the "science of imaginary solutions"', proposed at the beginning of the century by the French writer Alfred Jarry. Flanagan's 'soft' sculptures of the mid- to late 1960s – fabric bags either filled with sand or into which plaster had been poured and allowed to set, or lengths of rope that snaked and curled around the floor, marking out, defining and colonizing the space as in *four casb 2'67, ring/1'67, rope (gr 2sp 60) 6'67* (1967) – incorporated *ad hoc*-ism as a formal principle and not, as in the US, as an index of the happenstance of the real world.

In Britain, the combination of attitudes prevalent in the US and in Europe was behind the remarkable diversity of response to the work of Anthony Caro, who was then teaching on the advanced sculpture course at St Martin's School of Art in London. Students during the 1960s included Gilbert (b. 1943) and George (b. 1942), Barry Flanagan, Bruce McLean (b. 1944), John Hilliard (b. 1945), Richard Long (b. 1945) and Hamish Fulton (b. 1946). The Dutch artist Jan Dibbets (b. 1941) was also there on a scholarship for a short time. All these artists responded in various ways to the openness of enquiry that the course allowed by producing work that contrasted greatly with the formal qualities of Caro's sculpture. For instance, Flanagan's *Pile 3* (1968), a pile of loosely folded pieces of coloured hessian, takes the layer of coloured paint applied by Caro to unify his finished pieces, but mixes it with the staining of Louis and Noland and Minimalist techniques of arrangement.

The Summer 1967 issue of *Artforum* that crystallized the debate around Minimalism contained Fried's 'Art and Objecthood' and Sol

54 Barry Flanagan *four cash 2'67, ring/1'67, rope (gr 2sp 60) 6'67* 1967

LeWitt's 'Paragraphs on Conceptual Art'. Although 'Concept art', an art composed of ideas, had been mooted by the artist Henry Flynt (b. 1940) as far back as 1960, an art of that kind now seemed an increasingly realizable possibility within the 'complex and expanded field' opened up by Minimalism. 'In conceptual art', wrote LeWitt, 'the idea or concept is the most important aspect of the work. When an artist uses a conceptual form of art, it means that all of the planning and decisions are made beforehand and the execution is a perfunctory affair. The idea becomes a machine that makes the art.' The link between idea and finished work is evident in the deadpan descriptive titles LeWitt gave his works: *Ten thousand lines, five inches long, within an area of 6¾ x 5½ inches* (1971), for example, or *Four basic kinds of straight lines and their combinations* (1969). In some ways, then, Conceptual art continues what has already begun. The serialism is there, as is the understanding that the final artwork should not be subordinate to or illustrative of something else.

56

The idea of a process of preplanned moves suggests a connection between Conceptual art, mathematics and philosophy. LeWitt, though, insisted that 'conceptual art doesn't really have much to do with mathematics, philosophy or any other mental discipline. The mathematics used by most artists is simple arithmetic or simple number systems. The philosophy of the work is implicit in the work and it is not an illustration of any system of philosophy.' This echoes the rationale behind Mario Merz's use, since 1970, of the Fibonacci sequence of numbers, in which each number is the sum of the preceding two. The beginning of the sequence – 1, 1, 2, 3, 5 – is what Merz calls 'biologically thinkable. ...For example, we have one nose, two eyes, five fingers, precisely according to the series.' From this root in the body of the individual, the sequence's 'rapid and controllable expansion' spreads to encompass everything. For LeWitt, the idea from which the work issues was not sufficient in itself. It was first and foremost the idea to make *that* artwork; its strength, or lack of it, is not revealed until the work is complete. This need to complete things helps to make sense of LeWitt's insistence that, in spite of any impression given that Conceptual art is overly rational or predictable, it remains intuitive.

As with Minimalism, though, the act of making did not require LeWitt to lay his hands upon material and transform it himself. A wall drawing for which the instructions were 'Ten thousand lines not short, not straight, crossing and touching' could be executed by any number of people. In each case the drawing would 'look' different, but in each specific instance it would be an expression of LeWitt's idea (in the sense that a gene, as a set of coded instructions, is expressed). LeWitt began executing wall drawings in 1968. Sticking a drawing on paper onto the wall was fine, but drawing directly onto the brick or plaster of the available surface made the drawing more thoroughly a part of the architecture of the space. Working with similar preoccupations, the monochrome panels of masonite by Robert Mangold (b. 1937) functioned more as fragments for a putative remodelling of the gallery space than paintings, and, for a 1967 exhibition, William Anastasi (b. 1934) hung canvases in New York's Dwan Gallery carrying screened images of the walls they covered.

Nevertheless, there remains the thought that Conceptual art was somehow unexpressive. LeWitt spoke positively of making a thing 'emotionally dry' in order for it to be 'mentally interesting' for the spectator, and the French artist Daniel Buren (b. 1938) referred to an art that was 'impersonal'. Buren, who adopted the candy stripe as a

55 Niele Toroni
Présentation: imprints of a
no. 50 brush repeated at
regular intervals of 30 cm
1966–96

sign of art's presence, quoted and emphasized the French writer
Maurice Blanchot's phrase, 'a work of art of which nothing can be
said, except that it is'. His constant use of the stripe began with his
1966 agreement with Niele Toroni (b. 1937) and Olivier Mosset
(b. 1944) that each would make one painting over and over again,
whatever the situation. As true to the agreement as Buren, Toroni
has continued to cover his surfaces with evenly spaced dabs of a
broad, flat brush. The lawyer and critic Michel Claura noted in 1967
that this tactic called into question another cornerstone of the artistic
edifice built upon the need for originality and innovation. He wrote:
'In order to discuss a forgery, one must refer to an original. In the
case of Buren, Mosset, Toroni, where is the original work?'

71

Four basic kinds
of straight lines;
1. Vertical
2. Horizontal
3. Diagonal l. to r.
4. Diagonal r. to l.
and their combinations
S. LeWitt 1969

56 Sol LeWitt *Four basic kinds of straight lines and their combinations* 1969

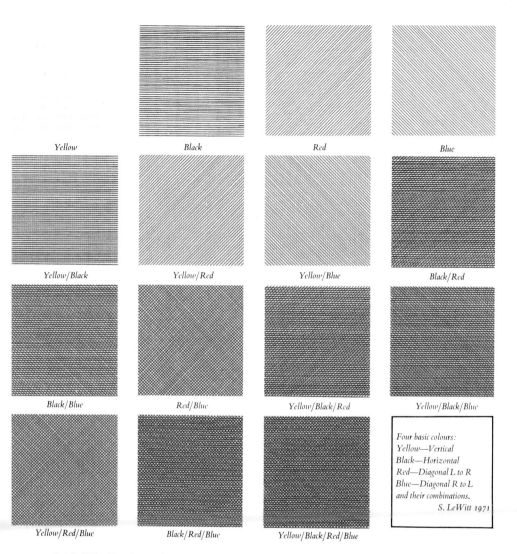

Yellow   Black   Red   Blue

Yellow/Black   Yellow/Red   Yellow/Blue   Black/Red

Black/Blue   Red/Blue   Yellow/Black/Red   Yellow/Black/Blue

Yellow/Red/Blue   Black/Red/Blue   Yellow/Black/Red/Blue

Four basic colours:
Yellow—Vertical
Black—Horizontal
Red—Diagonal L to R
Blue—Diagonal R to L
and their combinations.
                    S. LeWitt 1971

57 Sol LeWitt *Four basic colours and their combinations* 1971

73

Their tactic was adopted in order to achieve a 'position indispensable to the questioning process'. Buren was particularly concerned with the question of art's presentation, with where it could be placed and what consequences might follow from the choice of different sites: a domestic, commercial or gallery space, for example, or an exterior rather than an interior position, such as a wall or a billboard. Enquiries of this sort led to a redrawing of the artwork's boundaries. In March 1970, Buren had a blue and white striped poster included in the upper right hand corner of the Arts & Entertainments advertising panel in over 130 stations of the Paris Metro. Although done on the occasion of the '18 Paris IV 70' exhibition, 'these pasted pieces of striped paper', Buren wrote, 'were and still must be considered as part of a work which began, was carried on and is still in process outside and beyond the place and time of this particular proposal'. Furthermore, the posters provided the 'pretext' for a set of photographs, published as the book *Legend I*, which itself could only be 'a partial representation of what is (only) a fragment of a work in progress'. Buren's point was not that it would be difficult to see his work in its entirety, but that it would be impossible. The understanding of art as a set of products can be seen here to give way to the idea of it as a process that is coextensive temporally with the life of the artist and spatially with the world in which that life is lived.

58 Daniel Buren *Opéra* from *Legend I* 1970

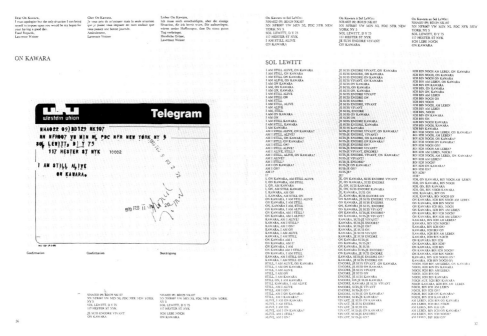

59 On Kawara *I am still alive* and a response from Sol LeWitt 1970

The contribution of Robert Barry (b. 1936) to the Düsseldorf exhibition 'Prospect 69', a question and answer text, made similar assumptions:

Q: Which is your piece for Prospect 69?
A: The piece consists of ideas which people will have from reading this interview.
Q: Can this piece be shown?
A: The piece in its entirety is unknowable because it exists in the minds of so many people. Each person can really know only that part which is in his own mind.

In the same spirit, the Japanese artist On Kawara (b. 1933) made his art from the 'historical fact' of his life. From the mid-1960s, his paintings have merely recorded the date on which they were executed. In accord with this matter-of-factness, Kawara's communications would also do no more than baldly confirm his continued existence: 'I am still alive. On Kawara.'

As the thrust of Buren's enquiries implies, Conceptual art concerned itself to a great degree with an examination of what art was: what were the necessary and sufficient characteristics required for a thing to be deemed art, and how might it be exhibited, curated and criticized? For some, this kind of examination remained a necessary activity prior to the making of art, while others considered that the enquiry itself constituted their art. Boundaries had once seemed more certain than this. There was art, which was one thing, and there were the things people said and wrote about it, which were another. Where Minimalism had found the meaning of an art object to lie to a certain extent 'outside' itself in its relationships with its surroundings, Conceptualism drew the tasks of criticism and analysis into the realm of art-making. What complicates the matter is that by this time a number of artists had begun to use language itself as a material. Conceptualism is often identified as a period during which art became insubstantial. Where there had once been paintings and sculptures, there were now items of documentation, maps, photographs, lists of instructions and bits of information in the work of among others Douglas Huebler (b. 1924), Robert Barry, Mel Bochner, Stephen Kaltenbach, Edward Ruscha, John Baldessari (b. 1931) and Victor Burgin (b. 1941). As Lawrence Weiner (b. 1942) and Joseph Kosuth (b. 1945) demonstrated in their different ways, however, even words have a quiddity which it is perfectly proper for the visual artist to investigate. Weiner, in a 1969 interview, considered the subject matter of his work to be materials, even though what was there to be seen in a gallery would be no more than a text naming substances and/or objects and what might be done with them: *One standard dye marker thrown into the sea* (1968), or *A 36" x 36" removal to the lathing or support wall of plaster or wallboard from a wall* (1968). Additionally, Weiner refused to make assumptions about the viewer, always accompanying his texts with the following short statement:

1. The artist may construct the piece.
2. The piece may be fabricated.
3. The piece need not be built.
   Each being equal and consistent with the intent of the artist, the decision as to condition rests with the receiver upon the occasion of receivership.

Effectively, the work according to Weiner 'can be presented just in language', and the options given to the viewer are important because

60 Lawrence Weiner *A 36" x 36" removal to the lathing or support wall of plaster or wallboard from a wall* 1968

'art is always a presentation. It is never an imposition.' Again we find discomfort with the concept of art as the expression of an idea or emotion belonging to the artist. Rather than asking what a piece means, that is, trying to work out what the artist is trying to tell us, it is now more appropriate for the 'receiver' to consider in what ways the information given could be meaningful. In like manner, Douglas Huebler could make a piece which designated a place, a particular site in New York, by locating a number of points. What can be done with this information by the viewer is left entirely open: 'I think "here it is" and that's all.' The piece cannot be experienced per-ceptually, but 'can be totally experienced through its documenta-tion'. For the exhibition 'January 5–31, 1969', organized by Seth Siegelaub in New York, Huebler exhibited photographs taken on a trip from Massachusetts to the city, not framing them but placing them in plastic sleeves on a window ledge. The images of *Site Sculpture Project, 50 Mile Piece, Haverhill, Mass. – Putney, Vt. – New York City* (1968) are evidence of, or ephemera relating to the journey rather than intentionally finished things in themselves.

61

61 Douglas Huebler *Site Sculpture Project, 50 Mile Piece, Haverhill, Mass. – Putney, Vt. – New York City* 1968

SITE SCULPTURE PROJECT
50 Mile Piece
Haverhill, Mass. – Putney, Vt. – New York City

1. Massachusetts Route 125	5. Interstate Route 91 (Conn.)	10. Interstate Route 91 (Conn.)
2. New Hampshire Route 101	6. Wilbur Cross Parkway (Conn.)	11. Connecticut Route 15–44
3. Vermont Route 5	7. Merritt Parkway (Conn.)	12. Massachusetts Turnpike
4. Interstate Route 91 (Mass.)	8. Deegan Expressway (N. Y.)	13. Massachusetts Route 495
	9. Merritt Parkway (Conn.)	

This work is formed by thirteen photographs that serve to mark the location of the sites listed above (and marked in that sequence) which actually describe 50 mile intervals of highway space.

All photographs were taken fifteen paces from the edge of the road with the camera held above the site and at a right angle to it.

Marked October 1968   DOUGLAS HUEBLER

In February 1969, *Arts Magazine* published four interviews – with Lawrence Weiner, Robert Barry, Douglas Huebler and Joseph Kosuth – conducted by 'Arthur R. Rose', a pseudonym of Kosuth himself. That its adoption was an aspect of Kosuth's practice as an artist, rather than a convenient means to pursue a parallel career as a critic, is evident in the homage which the name pays to Marcel Duchamp's female *alter ego*, Rrose Sélavy ('Eros, c'est la vie'). Kosuth spoke, in his auto-interview, of what it meant to be an artist:

Being an artist now means to question the nature of art. If one is questioning the nature of painting, one cannot be questioning the nature of art. If an artist accepts painting (or sculpture) he is accepting the tradition that goes along with it. That's because the word 'art' is general and the word 'painting' is specific. Painting is a *kind* of art. If you make paintings you are already accepting (not questioning) the nature of art. One is then accepting the nature of art to be the European tradition of a painting–sculpture dichotomy.

In saying this, Kosuth was influenced by Ad Reinhardt (1913–67), an artist of the Abstract Expressionists' generation who, for most of the decade up to his death in 1966, painted square, black paintings. These were not uniformly monochrome, however, but structured according to a broad, rectilinear cross design. Close inspection of each area of this pattern reveals different colours in the under-painting. 'Art is art as art,' Reinhardt had said, 'everything else is everything else.' What Kosuth drew upon was the way in which Reinhardt's critical and pedagogical activities around his painting had provided a context within which it might best be viewed and under-stood. His series of works, 'Art as Idea as Idea' pay homage to Reinhardt not only in their title, but also in their form, which

62 Joseph Kosuth *One and Three Chairs* 1965

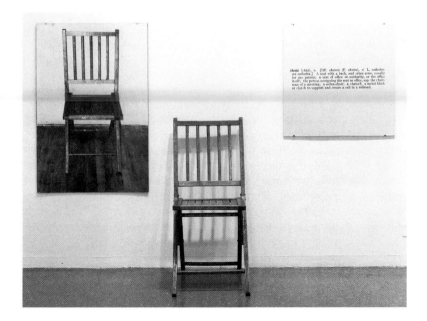

mimics the older artist's black paintings. Each work is a photostat of the dictionary definition of a word – 'art', 'idea', 'meaning', 'nothing' – blown up and printed in reverse, white out of black. Kosuth maintained that it was not the actual photostats that were art, but the ideas they represented: 'The words in the definition supplied the *art information*.' The definitions of 'Art as Idea as Idea' followed *One and Three Chairs* (1965), which comprises a wooden chair, a large black-and-white photograph of the chair and a photostat of the dictionary definition of the word 'chair'. Customarily the two wall-mounted elements would be seen as secondary facts, supporting and describing the primary object, the chair. What the piece asks, though, is whether we can be satisfied with that, or whether, in fact, the photograph and photostatted text do not themselves exist as chairs. To what extent can the photograph be relied upon as evidence of a state of affairs? It certainly appears to be an image of the real chair before us, but it might just as well be of another, almost identical item of furniture. If this were so its dependence upon the chair here is denied. The definition names the object before us, tells us what it is, but it also marks out a category of which the 'real' chair is only a single example.

In thinking about the interplay between reality, idea and representation, Kosuth drew heavily on the philosophy of Ludwig Wittgenstein, whose thoughts on the tautologous nature of mathematical propositions in his *Tractatus Logico-Philosophicus* were transferred to the field of art by Kosuth in his 1969 essay, 'Art After Philosophy'. He wrote: 'A work of art is a tautology in that it is a presentation of the artist's intention, that is, he is saying that that particular work of art is art, which means is a *definition* of art. Thus that it is art is true a priori (which is what Judd means when he states that "if someone calls it art, it's art").' A central idea of the *Tractatus*, that a proposition is like a picture of the world, appears widely applicable to 'dematerialized' art. As early as 1960 the French critic Pierre Restany had described Yves Klein's blue paintings as propositions. Mel Ramsden (b. 1944) an English artist working in New York in the late 1960s and early 1970s, made several paintings of texts stating facts about their own make-up, such as *100% Abstract* (1968): 'Copper Bronze Powder 12% / Acrylic Resin 7% / Aromatic Hydrocarbons 81%'. These were in the line of Morris's self-explanatory *Box with the Sound of its Own Making* (1961) and his 1963 self-cataloguing *File Card*. John Baldessari, working on the West Coast, employed a sign painter to put his laconic statements on canvas: *Pure*

62

EVERYTHING IS PURGED FROM THIS PAINTING BUT ART, NO IDEAS HAVE ENTERED THIS WORK.

ALL THE THINGS I KNOW BUT OF WHICH I AM NOT AT THE MOMENT THINKING— 1:36 PM; JUNE 15, 1969

Robert Barry

63 (above left) John Baldessari *Everything is purged from this painting but art; no ideas have entered this work* 1966–68

64 (above right) Robert Barry *All the things I know but of which I am not at the moment thinking – 1:36pm; June 15, 1969* 1969

Beauty, or *A painting with only one property*, or *Everything is purged from this painting but art; no ideas have entered this work* (all 1966–68). Terry Atkinson (b. 1939) and Michael Baldwin (b. 1945), two British artists, began working together in 1966. An early work, *Map to not* 65 *indicate* (1967), showed a rectangular area containing the outline of Iowa and Kentucky together with a list of all those surrounding states, provinces and areas of sea which are not in evidence. Their status as absent is akin to the situation described in Barry's piece *All the things I know but of which I am not at the moment thinking – 1:36pm; June 15, 1969*.

The collaboration between Baldwin and Atkinson led in 1968 to the establishment, with Harold Hurrell (b. 1940) and David Bainbridge (b. 1941), of Art & Language. All four taught in Coventry at the time, developing and running an art theory course at the art school. In their writings and discussions, which themselves constituted the 'work' of A&L, they addressed with a severely critical eye the recent developments in art and their implications for the

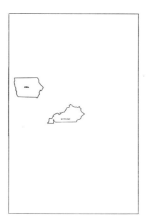

Map to not indicate: CANADA, JAMES BAY, ONTARIO, QUEBEC, ST. LAWRENCE RIVER, NEW BRUNSWICK, MANITOBA, AKIMISKI ISLAND, LAKE WINNIPEG, LAKE OF THE WOODS, LAKE NIPIGON, LAKE SUPERIOR, LAKE HURON, LAKE MICHIGAN, LAKE ONTARIO, LAKE ERIE, MAINE, NEW HAMPSHIRE, MASSACHUSETTS, VERMONT, CONNECTICUT, RHODE ISLAND, NEW YORK, NEW JERSEY, PENNSYLVANIA, DELAWARE, MARYLAND, WEST VIRGINIA, VIRGINIA, OHIO, MICHIGAN, WISCONSIN, MINNESOTA, EASTERN BORDERS OF NORTH DAKOTA, SOUTH DAKOTA, NEBRASKA, KANSAS, OKLAHOMA, TEXAS, MISSOURI, ILLINOIS, INDIANA, TENNESSEE, ARKANSAS, LOUISIANA, MISSISSIPPI, ALABAMA, GEORGIA, NORTH CAROLINA, SOUTH CAROLINA, FLORIDA, CUBA, BAHAMAS, ATLANTIC OCEAN, ANDROS ISLANDS, GULF OF MEXICO, STRAITS OF FLORIDA.

prevailing theories of modernism. The relationship between 'art' and 'language' for the group was never a straightforward one of form and material, practice and interpretation, and certainly not of image and commentary. The two were much more intimately bound up within a discourse carried on by a collective whose individual members 'sought not to be the authors of [their] work so much as agents in a practice which produced it'. For them the formalist stance taken by Greenberg, far from being the most persuasive *consequence* of the kind of art it championed, could better be understood as an expression of the values and expectations that produced the art in the first place. The French theorist Michel Foucault, most responsible for elaborating

SCHEMA:

(Number of)	adjectives
(Number of)	adverbs
(Percentage of)	area not occupied by type
(Percentage of)	area occupied by type
(Number of)	columns
(Number of)	conjunctions
(Depth of)	depression of type into surface of page
(Number of)	gerunds
(Number of)	infinitives
(Number of)	letters of alphabets
(Number of)	lines
(Number of)	mathematical symbols
(Number of)	nouns
(Number of)	numbers
(Number of)	participles
(Perimeter of)	page
(Weight of)	paper sheet
(Type)	paper stock
(Thinness of)	paper
(Number of)	prepositions
(Number of)	pronouns
(Number of point)	size type
(Name of)	typeface
(Number of)	words
(Number of)	words capitalized
(Number of)	words italicized
(Number of)	words not capitalized
(Number of)	words not italicized

65 (above left) Terry Atkinson and Michael Baldwin
Map to not indicate 1967

66 (below left) Art & Language
Index 01 1972 (partial view)

67 (right) Dan Graham
Schema 1966

'Schema' 1966 Daled Collection, Brussels

the idea of discourse during this period, described it more completely as not only the sum of statements made (or in this case, works of art produced), but also the operations of those institutions – here, museums and galleries, the art market, criticism and publishing – which provide the framework within which they are seen and are able to have an impact. Much as Art & Language saw Greenberg as in a real sense 'responsible' for Post-painterly Abstraction, Foucault described discourses as 'practices that systematically form the objects of which they speak'. *Index 01*, exhibited at Documenta V in 1972, included texts and charts pasted around the walls of a room in which stood eight filing cabinets full of closely cross-referenced excerpts from a range of theoretical texts. This was art that could not bestow idle visual pleasure, but which demanded work from the viewer. Art

& Language, though, were not aiming at obscurantism for its own sake, but at resisting the easy assimilation of their work into a comfortable 'story of art'.

In 1969, Art & Language published their journal, *Art-Language*, the first issue of which contained essays by members of the group and contributions from the Americans LeWitt, Weiner and Dan Graham (b. 1942). Graham, who had previously published an article in the magazine *Arts* drawing comparisons between Minimalism's modularity and the forms and arrangements of homes in suburban America, submitted the reflexive *Schema* (1966) which listed the number and type of words, numbers and other symbols contained in its own layout, along with information about the paper stock on which it was printed. The connection between Art & Language's project and the activities of some artists in New York, notably Kosuth, Christine Kozlov (b. 1945), Ramsden, and the Australian Ian Burn (1939–1993), led for a short while in the early 1970s to the establishment of an Art & Language there.

The documentary aspect of much Conceptual art, of course, lent itself to magazine publication. *Artforum* had been the main source of information but was by no means unique. In addition to several other US publications, in Europe there were *Art International*, published in Switzerland, *Interfunktionen*, in Germany, and a revitalized *Studio*, now dubbed *Studio International*, in Britain. Publications could deliver not just a picture of an artwork that existed elsewhere, or some news about it, but, in the case of work which comprised textual and photographic elements, the actual artwork. In 1970, *Studio* made use of this, producing an exhibition in the form of a book whose pages had been curated by six invited critics. The curator Seth Siegelaub, in particular, concentrated on this aspect of Conceptual art, organizing a number of exhibitions that existed primarily in catalogue form.

The ease with which information could be circulated contributed to the internationalism of Conceptual art. In his catalogue introduction to the 'Information' show at the MOMA in New York in 1970, the curator Kynaston McShine made a point of remarking on the show's inclusion of artists from Brazil, Canada and Argentina. Comments by the Brazilians Cildo Meireles (b. 1948) and Helio Oiticica (1937–80) reiterated this view and interpreted the terms of their participation as being of a similar nature to their art. The art was what it was, and not a representation of anything else; they, too, were who they were, and were not there as representatives of their country.

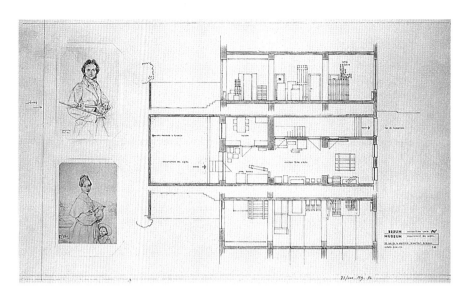

68 Marcel Broodthaers *Musée – Museum* Ex 73/100 1972

Conceptual art proposed that images can be recognized as being language-like: an artwork can be read. The reverse is equally true: words can work in a picture-like way. An older instance of this is Magritte's painting *The Treason of Images* (1929), a picture of a pipe beneath which appear the words 'This is not a pipe.' Marcel Broodthaers (1924–76), also a Belgian, made constant reference to his fellow-countryman's 1929 painting in his own work. Broodthaers was a poet, but observing, as he said, that artists were doing the same thing as him with the significant difference that they were making money, he had decided to become an artist. His first act was to make a sculpture, *Pense-Bête* (1964), by embedding the remaining copies of an edition of his poetry in plaster. Word and object remained closely connected in his work thereafter.

In the four years between 1968 and 1972, Broodthaers's work provided an extended critique of the museum system. It took the form of a fictional 'Museum of Modern Art', whose different departments came into existence as he staged successive exhibitions. The first section, the Department of Eagles, Nineteenth Century Section, was sited in his Brussels flat. It was a collection of crates, postcards and texts. 'This invention,' he said, 'a jumble of nothing, shared a character

85

connected to the events of 1968, that is, to a type of political event experienced by every country.' The largest section, seen at the Düsseldorf Kunsthalle in 1972, contained over 250 artefacts borrowed from collections around the world. Each exhibit depicted an eagle, the widespread symbol of power and authority, and emblem of Broodthaers's own museum. The way in which he organized these objects cut across normal systems of classification such as age, geographical location or function, and questioned how far the rationale of such groupings might contribute to the meanings of the individual items which they contain. Ordinary museums, relying on classification, are only able to present one form of the truth: 'To talk about this museum', said Broodthaers, 'means speaking about the conditions of truth.' Beside every item in his display he placed a label stating in either French, German or English: 'This is not a work of art.' This was meant as a challenge to the imagination: could these things, having once been designated as art by the system, be 'thought' back into the flow of reality from which they were plucked?

Arte Povera, impoverished art, was a phrase coined by the Italian critic Germano Celant in 1969, to describe the work of his countrymen Michelangelo Pistoletto, Alighiero e Boetti (1940–94), Giuseppe Penone (b. 1947), Giovanni Anselmo, Luciano Fabro (b. 1936), Giulio Paolini (b. 1940), Pino Pascali (1935–68), Gilberto Zorio, Mario and Marisa Merz, Pier Paolo Calzolari (b. 1943) and Jannis Kounellis (b. 1936). Art objects had hitherto been fashioned as the repository for emotions and ideas, 'a procedure', according to Celant, 'along binary parallels, art and life, in quest of the intermediate value'. In contrast, Arte Povera was 'the convergence of life and rich art', that paid more attention to 'facts and actions'. It was, '...almost a rediscovery of aesthetic tautology: the sea is water, a room is a perimeter of air, cotton is cotton, the world is an imperceptible ensemble of nations, an angle is a convergence of three coordinates, the floor is a portion of tiles, life is a series of actions'.

There were close affinities between Arte Povera's factual treatment of materials and the three-dimensionality of US art. A sense of the literal immediacy of materials, however, was achieved neither at the expense of their historical or poetic resonance, nor of their meta-phoric or symbolic potential. Celant's 'convergence' was the meeting of an ordered past with the contingent jumble of the present. Pistoletto's *Venus of Rags* (1967) juxtaposed the smooth perfection of a Classical nude statue – a composed, integral, halcyon ideal – with

73

69 (above) Jannis Kounellis
Horses 1969

70 (right) Giuseppe Penone
Twelve Metre Tree 1970

the chaos of a heap of fabric scraps. As here, Italy's past weighs heavily in much Arte Povera work. The outline of the country appeared frequently in Fabro's art, suspended upside down. It was, he said, necessary to discover the order of things, 'to induce the causes of the effects that are felt', rather than to search for essences. Paolini's search for order led to the frustration or dismantling of previous systems – Renaissance perspective, the rhythms of a Baroque façade, for example – in his mixed media works. The effects of natural processes and time on materials figured in Penone's *Twelve Metre Tree* (1970), and similar works that teased saplings from the trunks of mature trees. Anselmo extended the period under consideration in pieces that relied on the relative durability of granite and iron. *For an Incision of an Indefinite Thousands of Years* (1969) was a steel bar leant against the wall. Greased, and hence protected at its top end, the clean bottom half was open to the air and prone to oxidation. Ultimately the bar would disintegrate and slowly sink down the wall, inscribing a mark with its top edge as it did so. The two smooth granite blocks of *Untitled* (1968–86), one small, the other larger, were tied tightly together with vegetables squashed in between them. As the vegetables aged, shrivelled and dried up, the smaller stone, released from its binding, would fall to the floor. Regular replenishment was therefore required.

The conjunction and interaction between inert and organic matter, implicit in the sensuous form of Penone's 'Soffi' ('Gusts') – a

71 (left) Mario Merz *Igloo de Giap* 1968

72 (left) Giovanni Anselmo *Untitled* 1968–86

73 (above) Michelangelo Pistoletto *Venus of Rags* 1967

series of large hollow clay pots which he began in 1978 – were also characteristic of Kounellis's work. A multi-part untitled piece of 1967 comprised four troughs planted with living but slow-growing cacti, a metal bin stuffed to overflowing with recently grown and harvested raw cotton, and a rod protruding from a wall-mounted metal panel on which perched a macaw. For a 1969 exhibition in Rome eleven horses were tethered in the gallery. Fire as a purifying or transforming presence, or as a sooty trace, was also used regularly in association with the coal, sackcloth and metal of an industrial past, or with sculptural fragments redolent of lost cultural origins. The latter had a particular significance for the Greek-born Kounellis, a wanderer steeped in and yet removed from his past. Merz, in fact, made most obvious use of the notion of the artist as wanderer with his igloos. Writing of these structures, some made of soft materials, others, such as *Objet Cache Toi* (1968), from jagged-edged sheets of glass clamped to metal frames, Celant said: 'A shelter and a cathedral of survival, from the politics of art as much as from the winds, such

69

buildings are also the image of the nomad or vagabond, who does not believe in the secure object, but in the dynamic contradiction of life itself.'

Arte Povera challenged the settled order of things, and valued more the processes of the artist's life which sought poetry in the presence of materials, than objects offering meaning alone. The viewer of these works of art, confronted with the fact of their existence, ought to feel equally free to explore the information they offered.

Richard Long made art by going for walks. A route which could be easily conceptualized – a line, circle or square – would be followed on the ground. The walk itself could not be directly experienced by an audience who instead saw some form of documentation of it: a map with the route of the walk drawn on it, a text listing things passed or seen *en route*, a photograph, a tabulation of the walk as the carrying of a found object until such time as another was spotted and substituted, and so on. The preplanned logic of many of these was close to the sensibility of Conceptualism: *A Six Day Walk Over All Roads, Lanes and Double Tracks Inside a Six Mile Wide Circle Centred on the Giant of Cerne Abbas* (1975). Equally, Long might stop during the walk and make a line or circle with loose sticks or stones or by scuffing the ground with his boots. These would be left to disintegrate under the forces of nature and thus could only really be seen, too, as a photograph on a gallery wall. Working in a closely related way, although eschewing even the slight manipulation of the landscape undertaken by Long, Hamish Fulton would do no more than take a photograph in the course of a walk, or produce a text, either of which could be exhibited in a gallery on his return. In the face of such work the question 'Where is the art?' is often posed. Is the photograph *Walking a Line in Peru* (1972), for example, a work in its own right, or is there, somewhere in the Andes, a real work by Long of which we in the gallery see only documentary evidence? This conundrum is insoluble in terms of a logic which depends upon the primacy of the collectable art object, but the result of this should not be frustration at an inability to determine that here, and not there, is where the art lies. The options are not mutually exclusive, and, if there is a lesson in this, it is that the question had by now become irrelevant. The absence of an object from the gallery clearly identifiable as the 'artwork' encourages the notion that what we, as viewers, should be doing is deciding to look at the phenomena of the world in an 'art' kind of way. One would then be asking oneself the

74 Richard Long *Walking a Line in Peru* 1972

question: Supposing I look at this as if it were art. What might it then mean for me?

Long's walks could be seen in plain sculptural terms as a description of form in space, but there was another important strand to his work. Materials – slates, sticks, driftwood, mud – from a particular place might be removed and exhibited in a gallery. Here, the question is not so much 'Is the real work in the landscape or the gallery?' as 'What contribution does the landscape make to the particular effectiveness of the work in the gallery, given that the origin of the materials makes a difference?' From early on, Long was described as continuing in a specifically British tradition of landscape artists. His *England* (1967) is a photograph of a landscape in which a rectangular frame has been placed vertically in the foreground. Through it, another, circular one can be seen laid on a hillside in the distance. The treatment of framing, composition, viewpoint and perspective was something the work shared with Jan Dibbets's series of 'Corrected Perspectives', but it also calls to mind Andre's remark that the English landscape is the largest earthwork in the world.

75 Robert Smithson *Gravel Mirror with Cracks and Dust* 1968

Much more than Long or Fulton, the American Robert Smithson was concerned to develop a theory of the relationship between a particular location in the environment (which he called a 'site'), and the anonymous, essentially interchangeable spaces of the galleries in which he might exhibit (which he referred to as 'non-sites'). Among other things, sites had open limits, scattered information and were some place; non-sites, such as *Gravel Mirror with Cracks and Dust* (1968), had closed limits, contained information, and were no place, that is, were an abstraction. Because of the modular composition and geometrical simplicity of his first sculptures, Smithson was originally seen as a Minimalist, but even in these works his inspiration in crystal structure indicated that the 'impersonality' often attributed to Minimalism was not what he sought. Crystals occur naturally, and therefore thinking of simple geometrical forms as exclusively cultural *as opposed to* natural made little sense to him. That connection with nature and the environment would be a constant preoccupation. In the physical concept of entropy, the decaying of order into chaos, Smithson found a model for a practice that would result in some very large landscape interventions.

In contrast to Long and Fulton, Smithson's art and that of Walter de Maria (b. 1935) and Michael Heizer (b. 1944) demonstrated a preparedness to manipulate and alter the landscape on a far greater scale. One of Smithson's essays began: 'Imagine yourself in Central Park one million years ago. You would be standing on a vast ice sheet, a 4,000 mile glacial wall, as much as 2,000 feet thick. Alone on the vast glacier, you would not sense its slow crushing, scraping, ripping movement as it advanced south, leaving great masses of rock debris in its wake.' In comparison to forces of that magnitude, anything accomplished by an individual artist would be insignificant, and Smithson considered misplaced the growing sensitivity to environmental issues when it manifested itself as an exaggerated preciousness towards nature. *Partially Buried Woodshed* (1970) involved piling earth on top of a shed in the grounds of Kent State University until the central roof-beam cracked under the weight. The structure was then left. *Asphalt Rundown* (1969) was just that, truck-loads of asphalt poured down a slope outside Rome. Several other major works (including *Amarillo Ramp*, during the construction of which Smithson died in a plane crash in 1973), required the shifting of

76 Robert Smithson *Spiral Jetty* 1970

enormous quantities of rocks and earth. Most famously, his *Spiral Jetty* (1970) projected out from the shore into the Great Salt Lake made red by a particular type of algae. In the years since it was constructed, fluctuating water levels have first inundated and more recently revealed again the entire work.

For Smithson there was a close relationship between the formation and life of these sculptures – all of which, like Long's, were left to their fate – and mental activity. The laying of memory upon memory, the struggle to form a clear image from a jumble of impressions, and the connections made between disparate ideas and loss through forgetfulness all mirror sedimentation, folding, plate tectonics, seismic fracturing and other geological phenomena. Smithson would also document the environment as he found it, presenting, for example, photographs of the factory outflows, bridges and pontoons on the Passaic river in industrial New Jersey as a series of 'monuments'. In recognizing industrial structures as the true monuments to culture and civilization in the twentieth century, Smithson's attitude was close to the Germans Bernhard (b. 1931) and Hilla Becher (b. 1934) who had been photographing their 'anonymous sculptures' – water towers and pit-heads – since the late 1950s.

Until James Turrell (b. 1943) began working on an extinct volcanic crater in Arizona in 1972, the only other really large mover of earth had been Michael Heizer for his *Double Negative* (1969–70), a project in the Californian desert that drew formally on Heizer's father's experiences as an archaeologist working on pre-Colombian civilizations. On a more intimate scale, Walter de Maria's *50 m³ Level Dirt* (1968) filled Heiner Friedrich's Munich gallery to a depth of one metre. By no means all of the gallery could be seen from the doorway, so much of the work had to be either imagined or taken on faith, like the landscape from which its materials had been drawn. De Maria subsequently made two more versions of the work, the latest of which, *The New York Earth Room* (1977), uses 197m³ of earth and is permanently installed and maintained by the Dia Center for the Arts in New York. Dia also has on permanent display de Maria's *Broken Kilometer* (1979), which consists of 500 brass rods, each two metres in length, arranged on the floor in five parallel rows. This visible work is the companion piece to *Vertical Earth Kilometer*, a brass rod one kilometre long buried vertically in the ground outside the Museum Fridericianum in Kassel for Documenta VI in 1977. Also outside, de Maria used the floor of the Mojave desert on which to make a *Mile Long Drawing* (1968), and in New Mexico he placed

77 Bernhard and Hilla Becher
Typology of Water Towers 1972
(detail)

regularly spaced, vertical steel rods over an area of a mile by a kilometre to make his *Lightning Field* (1971–77). *Lightning Field* is permanent but isolated: 'Isolation', said de Maria, 'is the essence of Land
Art.' Those who wish to see it can do so in small groups, an over-
night stay in the nearby cabin allowing them sufficient time to make
the requisite walk around the area. The way in which the work is
seen is not extraneous to its condition and meaning, but part of it. In
his notes for the work, de Maria points out, for instance, that
viewing *Lightning Field* from the air would be of no value since the
relationship between sky and earth is so important; the centrality of
that relationship is clearly visible from the ground, especially when
the lightning so common in the area is forking through the air.

78

95

78 Walter de Maria
Lightning Field
1971–77

A contrasting art of the land was that of the Scottish poet Ian Hamilton Finlay (b. 1925) who, in 1967, moved to a croft outside Edinburgh. In the years since, among numerous other projects, he has turned the land and outbuildings there into a series of gardens to invite reflection on the mythical and historical dimensions of the art 81 of cultivation. The inscribed texts and carvings in and around Little Sparta are less impositions upon the land than incentives to read the landscape as an image of itself.

In 'Specific Objects', Judd had observed of sculpture that: 'since it isn't so general a form [as painting], it can probably only be what it is now – which means that if it changes a great deal it will be something else; so it is finished'. A decade and a half later, in 1979, the US critic Rosalind Krauss proposed a rationale for understanding the subsequent proliferation of art forms which, for want of a better word, continued to be grouped under the general heading of sculpture. Taking Morris's idea of the 'expanded field', Krauss argued that, for example, Land art might best be defined in terms of a double negative: it was neither architecture nor landscape. Furthermore, Krauss suggested, other works could better be placed in one of three other, related categories: landscape and architecture, architecture and not architecture, and landscape and not landscape. At first sight these seem merely self-contradictory, but when held up

79 Alice Aycock *A Simple Network of Underground Wells and Tunnels* 1975

80 Mary Miss *Untitled* 1973

81 Ian Hamilton Finlay
with Alexander Stoddart
Apollon Terroriste,
by the Upper Pool,
Little Sparta 1988

against much that was dubbed Land art, Environmental art and Installation, they started to make sense. The large wooden structures of the American artist Alice Aycock (b. 1946), *Maze* (1972) and *A Simple Network of Underground Wells and Tunnels* (1975), are not quite buildings, but are certainly more than the site on which they are constructed. Works by the American artists Nancy Holt (b. 1938) and Mary Miss (b. 1944) are additions to a place and yet serve essentially to reveal the landscape itself to the observer rather than to impose themselves upon it as a new presence. Miss's *Untitled* (1973) consists of a series of wooden panels placed one behind the other. A circular hole is cut in the first and an increasingly smaller segment in subsequent panels so that, when viewed end on, the hole appears to be sinking into the ground. The Manhattan skyline visible in the distance over the top of the panels ties the piece down, bringing about a 'complete integration between materials, idea, and place'.

Both 'Environmental' and 'Installation' are labels that have gained in currency since the 1970s to account for the increasing frequency with which spectators found that they had to be *in* an artwork in order to see and experience it. In America, the elasticity of

Environmental art has stretched to encompass de Maria's *Lightning Field* and Turrell's remodelling of Roden Crater, the large ecological projects of Helen (b. 1929) and Newton Harrison (b. 1932), and the gallery-contained eco-systems of Alan Sonfist (b. 1946) and Hans Haacke (born in Germany in 1936) as well as the spatial reworkings of Robert Irwin (b. 1928) and Michael Asher (b. 1943). In *Slant Light Volume*, for example, from a series of works from 1970 onwards, Irwin stretched sheer linen scrims of various colours across gallery spaces, changing the spectator's perception of their volumes through the least substantial means. Asher's piece for Pomona College in 1970 changed the gallery into two triangular rooms so that expectations of quality of light and sound as one moved away from the door were subtly confounded. Like Asher's work, the wall paintings of the German artist Blinky Palermo (1943–77) were site-specific and derived from the particular architectural details of the gallery that was to house them. A 1970 proposal for London's Lisson Gallery, for example, stipulated: 'A white wall with a door at any place surrounded by a white line of a hand's breadth. The wall must have right angles. The definite form of the line is directed to the form of the wall.'

The installations of the American artists Dan Graham and Bruce Nauman, sometimes using delayed video monitoring loops to place the spectator in two spaces at the same time, or Nauman's constructions such as his *Green Light Corridor* (1970–71), all surround the 83 spectator as architecture surrounds them, but in ways that belie and at the same time emphasize the functionality of 'real' architecture. Graham was interested in the links between architectural, built space and its phenomenal treatment in Minimalism. His pavilion-like structures, both inside and outside the gallery, use variously transparent and semi-mirrored glass, introducing the viewer to reciprocal vision, surveillance and self-reflection while walking around and through them. *Present Continuous Past(s)* (1974) introduced delay into 84 the video play-back between two mirrored rooms so that, by walking from one to the other, viewers could watch themselves being watched (see pp. 102–3).

There is so little space between the walls of Nauman's *Green Light Corridor* that one can scarcely do more than squeeze between them. That, though, is precisely what should occur. The work is not merely something to be looked at, but a space to be entered and experienced in a fully physical manner. Nauman's work took many forms, although all were rooted in his own bodily presence.

82 Bruce Nauman *Self-Portrait as a Fountain* 1966–70

83 (right) Bruce Nauman *Green Light Corridor* 1970–71

Reprising Duchamp's *Fountain*, the urinal readymade, he presented himself as the found object and photographed his upper body while spouting water from his mouth in *Self-Portrait as a Fountain* (1966–70). *Window or Wall Sign* (1967), a related work in neon, is equally ironic in its offering of the artist as a fount of aesthetic satisfaction. Set in a spiral, the text reads: 'The true artist helps the world by revealing mystic truths.' That the statement is ironic comes not only from its impossible idealism, but also from the juxtaposition of its idealism and the mundanity of Nauman's means. It is a reiteration, too, of LeWitt's assertion that art-making is in essence an intuitive process. In the late 1960s, he frequently used his body as a template for work, as well as focusing on other aspects of his identity: his signature, for example, rendered in neon but ludicrously exaggerated in one dimension or another. Nauman also undertook certain actions in his studio, recording them on video. These were very simple – walking in a particular way, pacing a square marked on the floor while playing the violin, bouncing two balls until he lost

Present continuous past(s) (1974)

The mirrors reflect present time. The video camera tapes what is immediately in front of it and the entire reflection on the opposite mirrored wall.

The image seen by the camera (reflecting everything in the room) appears 8 seconds later in the video monitor (via a tape delay placed between the video recorder which is recording and a second video recorder which is playing the recording back).

If a viewer's body does not directly obscure the lens' view of the facing mirror the camera is taping the reflection of the room and the reflected image of the monitor (which shows the time recorded 8 seconds previously reflected from the mirror). A person viewing the monitor sees both the image of himself, 8 seconds ago, and what was reflected on the mirror from the monitor, 8 seconds ago of himself which is 16 seconds in the past (as the camera view of 8 seconds prior was playing back on the monitor 8 seconds ago and this was reflected on the mirror along with the then present reflection of the viewer). An infinite regress of time continuums within time continuums (always separated by 8 seconds intervals) within time continuums is created.

The mirror at right-angles to the other mirror-wall and to the monitor-wall gives a present-time view of the installation as if observed from an 'objective' vantage exterior to the viewer's subjective experience and to the mechanism which produces the piece's perceptual effect. It simply reflects (statically) present time.

Photo showing installation of *Present Continuous Past(s)* at exhibition *Projekt (1974)* in Cologne, Kunsthalle. Subsequently the work was installed at ARC, Paris, 1974 and in 1974 at John Gibson Gallery, New York, at the *Institute for Contemporary Art*, Chicago, and at Wadsworth Atheneum, Hartford, Connecticut.
Collection: Musee National d'Art Moderne, Paris.

7

control, applying and removing make-up, manipulating a neon tube to examine the body in light and shadow – and were filmed in real time. They were neither scripted nor edited, but instead lasted just as long as it took to perform the task in question.

Video was a brand-new medium, Sony only bringing the first domestic equipment onto the market in the mid-1960s. One of the first to use the technology in his work was the Korean Nam June Paik (b. 1932). Paik had studied musical composition in Japan before moving to Germany and working with the musicians in the circle of Karlheinz Stockhausen (b. 1928), although his interest in randomness and chance events and his use of prepared and *ur*-instruments made from junk placed him much closer in spirit to Cage. In Germany, and later, New York, he became involved with Fluxus alongside its mix of artists, poets and composers including Beuys, Vostell, George Maciunas (1931–78), Dick Higgins (b. 1938), Alison Knowles (b. 1933), Yoko Ono (b. 1933), George Brecht (b. 1925), LaMonte Young (b. 1935) and many others. Paik's first video work in 1965 was

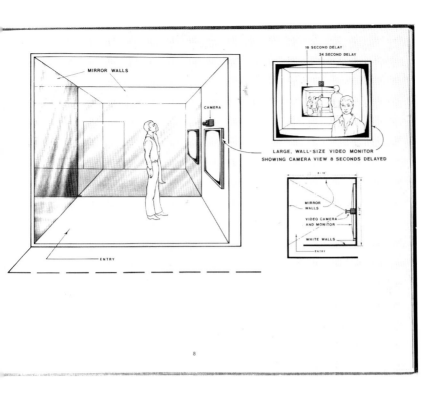

Labels within figure: MIRROR WALLS · CAMERA · ENTRY · 16 SECOND DELAY · 24 SECOND DELAY · LARGE, WALL-SIZE VIDEO MONITOR SHOWING CAMERA VIEW 8 SECONDS DELAYED · MIRROR WALLS · VIDEO CAMERA AND MONITOR · WHITE WALLS · ENTRY

84 Dan Graham *Present Continuous Past(s)* 1974

a film of Pope Paul VI's visit to New York made the day it was shown. He later produced many works that crossed between sculpture, Performance, music, video and TV, often in collaboration with the cellist Charlotte Moorman. He had been using TV sets – in *Zen for TV* and *Moon is the Oldest TV* (both 1963) – since the early 1960s, but his 1970s video installations *Fish Flies on Sky* (1975), a constellation of monitors on the ceiling, and *TV Garden* (1977), where monitors 'bloom' amidst lush green vegetation, involved and immersed the viewer to a far greater extent. Paik's snappily edited and colourful tapes such as *Global Groove* (1973) show that it is the medium of TV that shapes his work's content, and not the particular subject on the screen.

Once the emphasis in art had begun to shift from the end product to the process of its making, an acknowledgment of the bodily presence of the artist as a crucial factor in that process became all but unavoidable. Performance is that acknowledgment. Ad Reinhardt stated in an interview the year he died: 'I never go anywhere except as an artist.' Gilbert and George designated their whole life as art in a rather more overt manner: 'On leaving college and being without a penny, we were just there. ...We put on metallic make-up and became sculptures. Two bronze sculptures. Now we are speaking sculptures. Our whole life is one big sculpture.' Their first performances, in 1969, involved their appearance in public in just such a guise. *The Singing Sculpture* (1970) had the two of them, dressed smartly and with their faces and hands painted with metallic paint, standing on a pedestal miming to the Flanagan and Allen song 'Underneath the Arches'. Later performances strengthened not just the social, but the socializing aspect of the work: for example, they served dinner to David Hockney in front of an audience. From the early 1970s, they would indulge in evenings spent doing nothing more productive than getting drunk to be documented in multiple photo pieces: *Smashed* (1972–73), *Raining Gin* (1973), and so on. Under the slogan, 'Art for All', Gilbert and George offered themselves to their public again and again: 'With tears streaming down our faces we appeal to you to rejoice in the life of the world of art.' The question immediately arises as to whether this is guileless or ironic activity. Gilbert and George would maintain that they are being utterly sincere, but that might be a pose too. One solution to the problem might be to think of their work as both guileless *and* ironic: life paralleled or overlaid by an equally extensive representation of itself.

Such coextensiveness was one aspect of Performance. Throughout the 1960s, the Dutchman Stanley Brouwn (b. 1935) stopped passers-by, offering them a pad and pen with which to give him directions to a certain place. The instructions, useless as maps without his starting point and destination, and stamped *This Way Brouwn*, were then exhibited. Later he would account for his movement in other ways. During a trip to Czechoslovakia in 1972, for example, he recorded taking 150,815 steps, and in Poland 272,663. André Cadere (1934–78), a Romanian, had by the same year made his first *Barre de Bois Rond*. These bars were segmented, multicoloured rods which Cadere carried around and left propped up in a variety of art and non-art locations. They were, he said, 'exhibited in all places where [they were] seen: through any museum, placed in any exhibition by any artist, shown anywhere (street, underground, supermarket...)'. Cadere's statement appeared in *Studio* alongside a photograph of

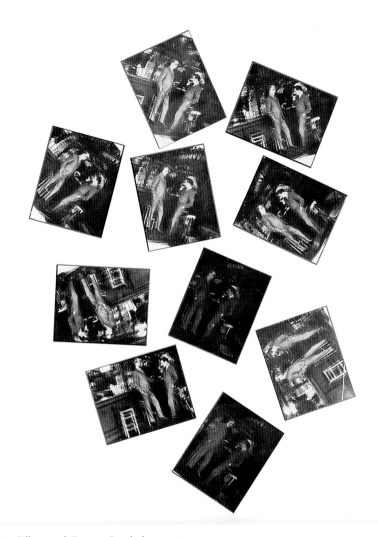

85 Gilbert and George *Smashed* 1972–73

himself holding one of his 'Barres'. The importance of documentation in this kind of work is different again to that in Conceptualism
or the Land art of Long and Smithson. Even when it takes place in a
gallery, a performance can only exist as a photograph or report for
everyone except the very few present as its audience.

The peculiar status of the photograph is most luridly illustrated by the critical fate of *Aktion 2* (1965) by the Viennese artist Rudolf Schwarzkogler (1941–69). Schwarzkogler was one of a number of Austrian artists – others included Gunter Brüs (b. 1938), Hermann Nitsch (b. 1938) and Otto Muehl (b. 1925) – whose ritualistic, often elaborate Performance works were termed Actionism. Nitsch's OM Theatre (Orgy Mystery Theatre) staged protracted rites involving large amounts of red dye, blood and the disembowelment of animals. They were, for Nitsch, 'an aesthetic way of praying'. Nitsch's actions were total experiences encompassing excessive stimulation of all the senses. Ritual had its place, too, in Schwarzkogler's art, as a defence against, or as a means of overcoming an otherwise irrevocable fragmentation and dissolution of the self. His first actions had been staged before an audience, but *Aktion 2* took place in private. Despite the privacy it remained an action, just as Nauman's video pieces were performances. Like Nauman, the Germans Reiner Ruthenbeck (b. 1937) and Ulrich Rückriem (b. 1938) had 'performed' solely for the video camera, as had Ulrike Rosenbach (b. 1944) in her 'Video Live Performances'. Using his friend Heinz Cibulka as the performer, Schwarzkogler set up tableaux that were to be photographed. In one image, Cibulka stands holding a gutted fish open in front of his genitals. Suggestive of both mutilated penis and open vagina, the fish's symbolism undermines the integrity or completeness of the sense of identity of the performer, Schwarzkogler's surrogate self. In another photograph, a fish-head is placed over Cibulka's penis.

Schwarzkogler died in 1969, and by the time his work became more widely known through its exhibition at Documenta V in 1972, the rumour mill had made the action and his death into one event. The critic Robert Hughes wrote of Schwarzkogler as 'the Vincent van Gogh of Body Art', who 'proceeded, inch by inch, to amputate his own penis, while a photographer recorded the act as an art event'.

The performances of the American Vito Acconci (b. 1940) explored similarly intense territory: he would bite himself, rub himself against the wall, lie under a platform masturbating while fantasizing about the people he could hear walking overhead and try to pull his chest out into the shape of a breast. In *Trappings* (1971), he spent three hours dressing his penis in doll's clothes and talking to it 'as a playmate'. Acconci described his activity as: 'Turning in on myself – dividing myself in two – attempting to turn my penis into a separate being, another person.' There was, in fact, much Body art and Performance that was excessive in one way or another. Largely, though, they came about as the result of working through an idea. Some were sensational: the paint-drenched performers in *Meat Joy* (1964) by Carolee Schneeman (b. 1939) rivalled Nitsch's spectacle, and the Californian Chris Burden (b. 1946) variously crawled across a floor strewn with broken glass, had himself shot and was crucified on a car. Barry Le Va hurled himself against a wall until he collapsed, exhausted. Dennis Oppenheim (b. 1938) had stones thrown at himself, and allowed himself to be badly sunburned. In Europe, aside from the Actionists of the 1960s and the related work of Peter Weibel (b. 1945), Arnulf Rainer (b. 1929) and Valie Export (b. 1940), there were the investigations of Gina Pane (1939–90) of the perennial *Vanitas* theme which often involved self-laceration. Stuart Brisley (b. 1933) in Britain, both alone and in collaboration with others, underwent severe trials of endurance while questioning social institutions, our incorporation into them and possible means of resistance to their hegemony. In the early 1980s, Brisley examined some aspects of Body art and Performance in the film *Being and Doing*, exploring

86 Vito Acconci *Trappings* 14 October 1971

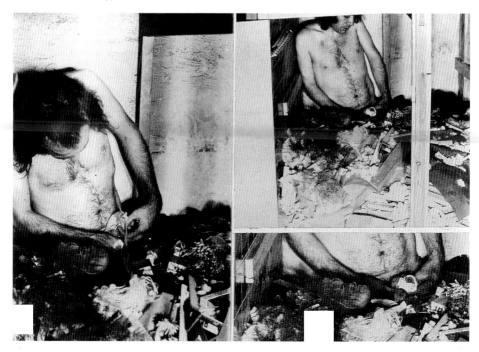

in particular the significance of the art form in Eastern European countries. Under such regimes, an artistic gesture which laid stress on the physical presence of the artist as an individual agent had a political dimension wholly absent in a Western social context.

The Serbian Marina Abramovic (b. 1946) pushed her body to its physical limits as a way of emptying it in readiness for a fuller spiritual experience. Her solo performances in the early 1970s, many called 'Rhythms' after prior work in sound installation, required her to shout until she was completely hoarse, to dance until she collapsed from exhaustion, be buffeted by a wind machine until she passed out, to flagellate herself, take mind-altering drugs and perform other perilous acts. Lying down in the centre of a fire in *Rhythm 5* (1974), she passed out through lack of oxygen and had to be rescued by onlookers. In her final 'Rhythm' performance, *Rhythm 0* (1974), she placed herself silently in the Studio Mona Gallery in Naples next to a table holding 72 varied objects. Visitors were invited to use them, and her, as they saw fit. Proceedings were halted when Abramovic, having had all her clothing cut from her, was forced to hold a pistol, placing the barrel in her open mouth. It was difficult to enjoy a ghoulish *frisson* of delight in front of these works since the risks Abramovic took with her own body placed such heavy responsibilities upon her audience. These responsibilities had less to do with saving her from herself than with the larger point – relevant to all Performance – that however committed an artist might be, such commitment is of little value unless it is met with equal involvement on the viewer's part.

87 Marina Abramovic *Rhythm 0* 1974

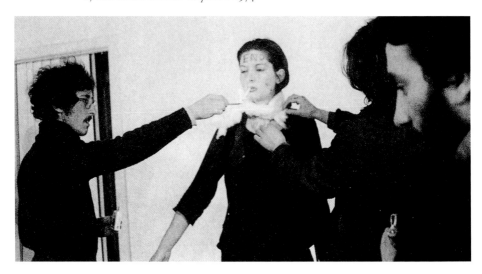

88 Joseph Beuys
*How to Explain Pictures to a
Dead Hare* 1965

   The matted, informal structure of felt made it ideal for Morris's purposes in his post-Minimal works. It was, though, a material already closely associated with the German artist Joseph Beuys. The story of Beuys's wartime experiences and how he was shot down without a parachute, rescued and kept alive by being smeared with fat and wrapped in felt to stay warm, had become an integral part of the mythic, almost shamanistic power of his art. Fat and felt remained his prime materials and although there were formal similarities between his work and that of the Minimal and post-Minimal artists – notably his *Fat-corner* (1960) and the space-altering

89 Joseph Beuys *Coyote, 'I like America and America likes Me'* 1974

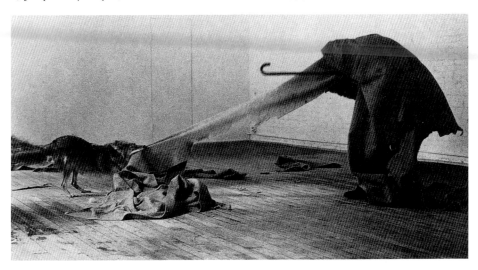

works of Flavin, Morris and Hesse – there were in other respects quite considerable differences. The greatest of these concerned Beuys's conception of himself as a 'transmitter'. The problem, as far as Beuys was concerned, lay not in the attempt to find an art practice appropriate to the changed circumstances of the world, but in communicating to an audience just what that art was about. He said, 'Sculpture must always obstinately question the basic premises of the prevailing culture. This is the function of all art, which society is always trying to suppress. ...Art alone makes life possible – this is how radically I should like to formulate it. I would say that without art man is inconceivable in physiological terms.' In 1965 he had

88 staged his performance, *How to Explain Pictures to a Dead Hare* in a gallery from which the audience were excluded. His head smeared with honey and covered with gold leaf, Beuys sat talking to the dead hare on his lap – because hares understand better than humans – while the audience could only observe through the window. In 1967, Beuys started a political party for animals, stating that their 'elemental energy' might well achieve more in the way of political innovation than any human. He was invited to contribute to Morris's 'Nine at Castelli' show in 1969, but declined. When he finally did show in New York, in 1974, it was in a manner which emphasized the necessity for and difficulty of achieving reciprocity in

89 communicative action. For *Coyote, 'I like America and America likes me'* (1974), Beuys had himself transported by ambulance, wrapped in felt, from the airport direct to René Block's gallery where he spent five days in an enclosure with a coyote before being carried back to the airport. Whereas the thrust of three-dimensional work was towards an openness within its environment that allowed interpretative activity on the part of the viewer, Beuys kept much more closely to the traditional idea of art as something which embodied or offered a particular meaning: 'If I produce something, I transmit a message to someone else. The origin of the flow of information comes not from matter, but from the "I", from an idea,' he said.

In more general terms, the distinction between American and German art of the period could also be demonstrated by a comparison between the character of Happenings and of Fluxus events. Both drew on Dada, but while Happenings were extensive, a multiplicity, full of things, Fluxus events were simple and unitary in conception. In addition, the 'anti-art' of the Fluxus artists, and this of course included Beuys, was aimed at reconnecting art with life in a fully political sense.

CHAPTER THREE

Ideology, Identity and Difference

The kind of art produced by Andy Warhol's Factory – depersonalized, mechanized, using multi-unit production processes – characterized the 'ideology' of most Pop art: art, like all industrial products manufactured for a capitalist market economy, was just a commodity and no more. The dealer's job was to create a market in which such commodities could be bought and sold. Faced with that reality, thoughts of beauty, aesthetic value and transcendent worth are irrelevant. Ultimately, a work of art is worth what someone is prepared to pay for it; concomitantly, the question as to what drives people to devote themselves to art finds an easy answer: they do it for the money.

Throughout the later 1960s and early 1970s, anything which fed a market and thereby contributed to the commercial well-being of the Western economies was perceived by some US artists in particular to be lending tacit support, however indirectly, to US involvement in, among other things, the Vietnam War. There was, therefore, an additional reason to explore the thoroughly non-mercenary nature of Conceptualism and the transience of Performance: an art which could assert itself as such, while denying the saleability of objects, carried a certain ideological and political efficacy that was contrary to the tenets of capitalist market economy.

Asked by *Artforum* to comment on 'the deepening political crisis in America' for a 1970 symposium the periodical published on 'The Artist and Politics', respondents offered a range of opinions on the relationship between the making of art, the issue of commitment, and a more direct involvement in political activity. The answers made explicit the belief of many artists whose work was radically abstract that their activities had clear political implications and overtones. Don Judd, Jo Baer, Carl Andre and Richard Serra, among others, explained how, and Baer also described how the political dimension of their activities implicated the spectator. She said: 'Works of art are no longer presented as a precious class of objects. Will a special class of subjects also be relegated to history?'

This recognition of the mutual responsibility of artist and spectator for any political meaning in art was at the opposite pole from the belief that, in order to instigate social change, art's messages should be simple and unambiguous. The way a work fitted into the successive history of objects was of less importance than the connections it forged with its context, and that context was as much political as it was spatial, visual or aesthetic. Artists, traditionally seen as unclubbable individualists, began to organize themselves into pressure groups, which carried further the idea prevalent within Conceptualism that it was the artist's responsibility to establish the context for his or her work as much as to make the work itself. Context now was more than the critical environment provided by the specialist magazines; it was the world at large. The Art Workers' Coalition (AWC), for example, was set up in early 1969. This group of members of the New York art community organized protests and representations not only about the war, but also about civil rights and the right of artists to be consulted about the way their work is displayed and deployed within the museum and gallery system. One of their demands, for instance, was the presence of a Puerto Rican on the board of any museum or gallery that might be expected to exhibit Puerto Rican art. Original members of the AWC included the critic Lucy Lippard, the Greek Kinetic and Sound artist Takis (b. 1925), Hans Haacke and Carl Andre. Haacke, born in Germany, had been living in New York for some years. His early work examined self-contained systems of an ecological or environmental nature, but by this time his focus had shifted to economic and social systems. Like many others, Haacke viewed Political art as a rejection of the formalist approach to practice and criticism espoused by Greenberg. He stated, 'For decades now [Greenberg's formalist doctrine] has managed to have us believe that art floats ten feet above the ground and has nothing to do with the historical situation out of which it grew. It is presumed to be an entity all to itself. The only acknowledged link with history is a stylistic one. The development of those 'mainstream' styles, however, is again viewed as an isolated phenomenon, self-generative and unresponsive to the pressures of historical society.'

Although Haacke produced work that was often extremely critical of the power brokers and vested interests of the art world, he chose to continue to show in the mainstream museum and gallery system since it was only there that his message was likely to have any impact. Using information freely available in the public domain, he conducted

90 Leon Golub *Interrogation II* 1981

in-depth analyses of the business dealings of those involved in the
arts. Looking at firms in the arms trade generously sponsoring the
arts, or whose investments in South Africa helped to prop up
apartheid, or revealing the oppressive work practices in factories
owned by one of Europe's leading art collectors, Haacke made the
links between art and commerce more visible. *Shapolsky et al.* 91
*Manhattan Real Estate Holdings, a Real-Time Social System, as of May 1,
1971* (1971) documented the large number of buildings in Lower
Manhattan owned and controlled by members of one family. Haacke
planned to include the work in his 1971 exhibition at the
Guggenheim Museum. The Guggenheim's director, Thomas Messer,
refused to accept the work on the grounds that it was not art, a decision that caused the cancellation of the entire exhibition. Haacke has
always been careful by whom his works are collected. His investigation

113

of the working conditions at the factory of Peter Ludwig, *The Chocolate Master* (1981), was not allowed to be sold to its subject. This was to prevent it being stored unseen in the basement of Cologne's Museum Ludwig, where the rest of the industrialist's large collection is housed.

This level of control over the fate of one's work contrasts with that of a deeply politicized artist like Leon Golub (b. 1922) whose paintings might be taken as comment on a particular conflict, but which speak more generally of the horrors of oppression and the abuse of power. From the 1950s onwards, successive series of paintings have been stimulated by examples of US military involvement, notably, as in *Interrogation II* (1981), in Asia and Latin America, and by social injustice and the civil rights struggle at home. In 1968, Golub was one of the group which tried to persuade Picasso to withdraw *Guernica* from display in New York's Museum of Modern Art: a work critical of German bombing of the Basques in the Spanish Civil War should not offer implicit support to the US bombing policy in Vietnam by remaining on show. But Golub, aware, as a member of society, of his own unavoidable complicity in these matters, is prepared to exploit the ambiguity of a person's position. On the one hand, the person who buys his paintings 'owns him', and 'takes possession of his mind'. Equally, however, the purchase means that the paintings enter the new owner's home and their message has to be confronted there. As he wrote, 'Even if they would glamourise it and even if they would give it a special aspect temporarily, I think the message is sufficiently clear that the violence in the work, the vulnerability in the work will have its effect.'

In 1967, Joseph Beuys started a student political party at the Düsseldorf Academy where he taught. This was one of the earliest organizational manifestations of his belief in the connections between learning, creativity and the social processes of change or revolution. Engaged in Mao-inspired activity and notable among his pupils at the time was Jörg Immendorff (b. 1945) who, under the aegis of his own *Lidl* 'academy', made a number of anti-establishment actions. By 1972, Beuys had been fired by the Academy for insisting, in line with his beliefs, that his classes be open to unrestricted numbers. A year later, he formed the Free International University, aimed at stimulating discussion across the boundaries of academic disciplines. Freed from the restrictions placed upon research by the political and economic imperatives of departmental operation, Beuys hoped that it might be possible to advance thinking on various issues by approaching them from a number of different theoretical viewpoints at once. The interdisciplinary approach of Beuys's FIU was also at the heart of John Latham's Artist Placement Group in Britain.

The organizers of the 'Information' show at the Museum of Modern Art, New York in 1970, had included a book-list at the back of the catalogue, the principal aim of which was to indicate further reading in and around art and art theory to explain the proliferation of materials and techniques available to the contemporary practitioner. By the time of 'Art into Society/Society into Art', an exhibition of German art including work by Beuys, Wolf Vostell, Dieter Hacker (b. 1942), K. P. Brehmer and Gustav Metzger (b. 1926) held at London's ICA in 1974, things had changed. The

91 Hans Haacke
Shapolsky et al. Manhattan Real Estate Holdings, a Real-Time Social System, as of May 1, 1971
1971

reading list had become an exercise in pedagogy, not only suggesting related writings on art, but also detailing texts by philosophers and political and cultural theoreticians including Adorno, Marx, Lukacs, Goldmann and Marcuse. Interest in the work of such authors was an aspect of the protracted debate during the 1970s over the correct relationship between art and politics, largely inspired by neo-Marxism. Could art communicate and be understood politically, or would any political function necessarily undermine its aesthetic purpose?

Much work was done at the time in analysing earlier modernist models, notably the conjunction of experimentalism amongst artists and social reconstruction following the Russian Revolution, and the exemplary work of political agitation undertaken by John Heartfield (1891–1968) in his anti-fascist photomontages of the 1930s. The modernist medium of photomontage was significant as a technique within socially concerned art practices; photography itself was considered to be important in analysing social reality. In the tradition of realist and reportage imagery – August Sander (1876–1964), Paul Strand (1890–1976), Diane Arbus (1923–71), and Margaret Bourke-White (1906–71) – it could be seen as an index of the real conditions of the world. Coupled to the kinds of visual analyses then being developed by critics of film, it seemed to offer even more. The various details in a photograph could be understood as signs in a visual language and therefore images could give up their meaning through being 'read', as the French theorist Roland Barthes had been exploring in his semiological analyses of media imagery since the 1950s.

Heartfield's techniques were borrowed heavily by, among others, the German Klaus Staeck (b. 1938) and the British artists Victor Burgin and Peter Kennard (b. 1949). Like Heartfield's, these artists' work was designed for the medium of print, conceived for mass production on cards, posters and in magazines, and distributed widely. For example, Kennard's work on Chile's 'Disappeared' and the economics of mineral exploitation that contributed to US involvement in Pinochet's overthrow of the Allende government was designed for, and appeared in, a 1978 issue of the photographic journal *Camerawork*. His subsequent work concentrated on social conditions in Britain and the Campaign for Nuclear Disarmament campaign against cruise missiles. Victor Burgin's 1978 poster of a young couple embracing, as if in an advertisement for diamonds, bore the copy line: 'What does possession mean to you? 7% of the population own 84% of the wealth.' Could work like this do anything more than reaffirm the distaste of those already unhappy with such statistics? If art were not capable of being straightforwardly instrumental in bringing about social change, in what might its effectiveness consist and how would that be measured? The necessity for an art that was realist 'for society', and by extension 'social realist', was pondered in the light of questions such as these, especially in view of the crudely propagandistic image that Soviet Socialist Realism had in the West.

One of the most important influences in some art and art criticism in the early 1970s was the impact of feminism. As we have seen, the relationship between the political viewpoint of a society and its art had been the focus of much attention already, mainly within a neo-Marxist theoretical framework. Whatever the rights and wrongs of the distribution of power among those who produce and those who own the means of production, the vast majority of players on both sides appeared to be men. Statistical information produced by early activists made the case in stark terms. In 1971, for example, the Los Angeles Council of Women Artists issued a statement pointing out that, over the previous ten years, of 713 artists who had exhibited in group shows at the Los Angeles County Museum, only 29 had been women. Over the same period the museum had mounted 53 one-person shows, only one of which had featured a woman. Similar ratios pertained in museums and galleries everywhere.

In New York, Women Artists in Revolution (WAR) had formed in 1969 out of the Art Workers' Coalition. The ambivalence with which its aims were greeted is exemplified by the response of Lucy Lippard, already a major critic and someone who would go on to become an important figure in the development of feminist critique. In the introduction to her 1976 collection of essays on women's art, *From the Center*, she recalls her early annoyance at the provocative partisanship of WAR and then, later, her acceptance of its significance. Of her previous book of essays, *Changing*, she wrote: 'All through *Changing*, I say "the artist, *he*," "the reader and viewer, *he*," and worse still – a real case of confused identity – "the critic, *he*."' What was recognized here was what almost amounted to a certain complicity on the part of women – however unwitting – in maintaining the *status quo*. The various strategies adopted in an attempt to remedy the imbalance of opportunity and reward in the art world relied, in the first instance, on separatism: a setting-up of projects, discussion groups, exhibitions and journals to be run exclusively by women for women, and in writing the history of women's art. It was recognized at the same time that elements within recent art, as well as culture generally, had to some extent paved the way for art's engagement with feminist consciousness. Lippard, for instance, saw: 'the seeds of my feminism in my revolt against Clement Greenberg's patronization of artists, against the imposition of the taste of one class on everybody, against the notion that if you don't like so-and-so's work for the "right" reasons, you can't like it at all, as well as against the "masterpiece" syndrome, the "three great artists" syndrome, and so forth'.

In 1971, the art historian Linda Nochlin published an essay posing the question, 'Why Have There Been No Great Women Artists?' In answering, she pointed to the curatorial practices of museum and gallery staff, and to the values inculcated and reinforced by art history. She wrote, 'A feminist critique of the discipline of art history is needed which can pierce cultural-ideological limitations to reveal biases and inadequacies not only in regard to the question of women artists, but the formulation of crucial questions of the discipline as a whole.'

The language of art history and criticism did not even acknowledge women in order to deny them. It assumed, rather, that women would simply not need to be considered. A great artist was an 'old master', and a great work of art was a 'masterpiece'. Within such an evaluative framework, 'genius', whatever that may be, becomes an exclusively male preserve. To perform a simple act of reversal and to think of accomplished women artists not as old masters but as 'old mistresses' was to reveal the completeness of male dominance in the field. It was so pervasive as to seem natural. In order to combat this, male dominance had to be explained as the outcome of social factors. The fight was on against such attitudes as those expressed, for example, on more than one occasion by the British sculptor Reg Butler (1913–81), who suggested that women made art, that is, were creative, only until such time as they could fulfil their true nature and be procreative. Art, for women, was a kind of stopgap, filling the time before children came along.

What feminism provided was a means of visualizing and discussing this issue without having to fall back on a simple nature/culture dichotomy. Through its critique of patriarchy, feminist theory emphasized that those polarities which appeared to characterize natural differences in the essential qualities of man and woman – intellect/intuition, day/night, sun/moon, culture/nature, public/private, outside/inside, reason/emotion, language/feeling – were only meaningful within culture. Where the real differences between them lay was in the play of power: who had it and who did not.

From the outset, a number of major initiatives made themselves felt. The first of these was an exercise in historical reclamation, the second a critique and reappraisal of the criteria of judgment, and the third a prolonged examination, through the production of further work, of how this activity called 'art' and this set of ideas referred to as 'feminism' might be related and how they might act reciprocally upon one another. First and foremost, there was a need to go back through the history of art to rediscover the work of those many women artists whose careers had been obscured through neglect and whose work had even been attributed to men on certain occasions. One had to visit the basements and storerooms of the major museums and pull out into the light all those works by women that had been relegated there because they were not deemed to be of sufficiently high quality to remain on permanent display, or because they were not adequately representative (i.e. were considered to be derivative of male work in the same style), and even because they dealt with the wrong kind of subject matter.

The large installation *The Dinner Party* (1974–79) by Judy Chicago   92 was conceived as just such an attempt at reclamation, 'a symbolic history of women's achievements and struggles'. In 1970, Judy Gerowitz placed a full-page advertisement in *Artforum*, appearing as a boxer in the ring and stating that, as the endemic male domination of the art world militated not only against the acceptance of her work but that of all other women artists, she would renounce the name given to her by her father and would henceforth be known, after the city of her birth, as Judy Chicago. Together with her colleague Miriam Schapiro (b. 1923), she set up the first Feminist Art Program at the California Institute for the Arts. Chicago had begun as a painter and, towards the end of the 1960s, had moved into making atmospheric works using coloured smoke in a way that paralleled the preoccupation with light and environment in the work of her West Coast contemporaries Robert Irwin, James Turrell and Larry Bell. The next move beyond that, which saw atmosphere not as an abstract, universalized space, but as something pervasively socialized and politicized, was something quite new. For a triangular table, a shape which both denied a hierarchical seating arrangement and suggested female sexual identity, Chicago designed 39 place settings, each celebrating the life and work of a famous woman. The needlework on the place mats and the images painted and glazed onto the plates reflected the achievements of the place settings' subjects. Underneath the table, the porcelain floor of golden triangles bore a further 999 names of 'supporting' women.

Related to work of this kind were several attempts to search out and establish an alternative spiritual legacy, one that would speak to the needs and desires of women rather than men. Was there, perhaps, some form of matriarchal social system, one watched over by goddesses, not gods, that could be seen to have preceded the current patriarchal domination of things? *God Giving Birth* (1968) by Monica Sjoo (b. 1942) is a straightforward and early example of this. Mary Beth Edelson produced a 'Great Goddesses' series (1975) of which she said: 'The ascending archetypal symbols of the feminine unfold today in the psyche of modern Everywoman. They encompass the multiple forms of the Great Goddess. Reaching across the centuries we take the hands of our Ancient Sisters. The Great Goddess, alive

92 Judy Chicago *The Dinner Party* 1974–79

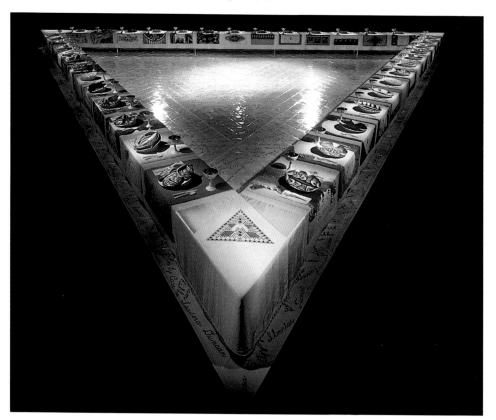

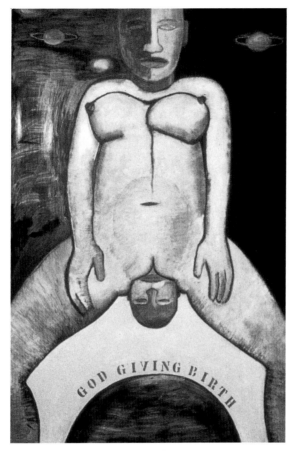

93 Monica Sjoo *God Giving Birth* 1968

and well, is rising to announce to the patriarchs that their 5,000 years are up. Hallelujah! Here we come.'

Eva Hesse had died in 1970 from a brain tumour, too early for her work to have been thought to be particularly influenced by feminist ideas. It did, however, provide a powerful example for those who wished to avoid Minimalism's cool impersonality, a trait that was increasingly being seen as indicative of masculinity. Hesse had retained Minimalism's modularity, but had used it in a very un-Minimalist way. Her work was not engineered but handmade, bringing a quite different bodily sense to the very similar but by no means

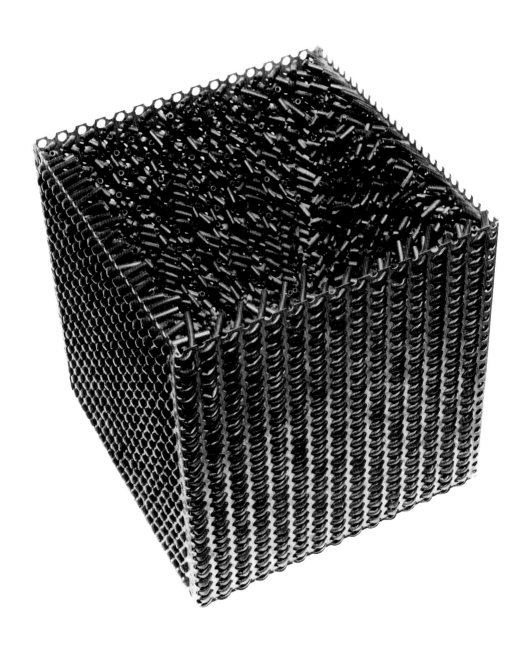

94 (above) Eva Hesse *Accession V* 1968

97 (far right) Harmony Hammond *Presence IV* 1972 ▶

95 (above) Nancy Graves *Paleo-Indian Cave Painting, Southwestern Arizona (To Dr.Wolfgang Becker)* 1970–71

96 (below) Louise Bourgeois *Fillette* 1968

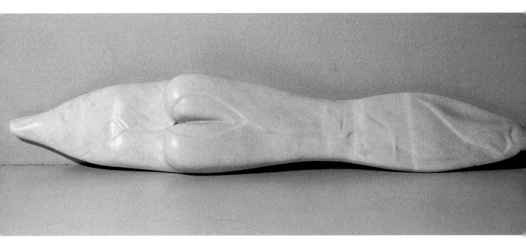

98 Louise Bourgeois *Femme Couteau* 1969–70

identical elements in her multi-part works. There was also an overt psychological dimension, for example, the lengths of plastic tubing threaded through the open cube of *Accession V* (1968), recalling the disturbing image of Meret Oppenheim's emblematic Surrealist object, the fur-covered cup and saucer of 1936. The sexuality of Hesse's forms was close in form to the sculpture of Louise Bourgeois (b. 1911). From an older generation, Bourgeois' eroticized works in marble, plaster and latex came to provide a richly inspirational resource for many women artists. Starting in the early 1960s, she had made a succession of works on the theme of the lair. Although enclosing and reassuring, these spaces could also become traps, and so always needed a second entrance at the rear to allow for escape. The phallic *Fillette* of 1968, hanging by its tip from a wire hook, and the soft folds and contours within the aggressive overall shape of *Femme Couteau* (1969–70) exemplify Bourgeois' constant drawing together of destruction and seduction. She wrote, 'These women are eternally reaching for a way of becoming women. Their anxiety comes from their doubt of being ever able to become receptive. The battle is fought at the terror level which precedes anything sexual.'

The grids of the Canadian artist Jackie Winsor (b. 1941) also made idiosyncratic use of Minimalism as in the case of Hesse. Regular in their pattern, they were nevertheless unpredictable due to Winsor's

94

96

use of irregular branches rather than planed wood. The repetitive unevenness of these grids has something of the 'anti-formalist structuring' spoken of by the American Nancy Graves (1940–95). More than the unsettlingly tender and diverse installations of Ree Morton (1936–77), Graves's mixed media works – *Paleo-Indian Cave Painting, Southwestern Arizona (To Dr. Wolfgang Becker)* (1970–71), for example – drew on social realities outside the male dominance of Western culture. As with Hesse, though, there is also a strong antecedent for her work in the gestural freedoms of Pollock's drip paintings, and the same was true of another American artist Harmony Hammond (b. 1944). Hammond constructed her 'Presences' from threads, hair and paint-covered strips of cloth torn from dresses. In these works, whose collective title expresses the desire to assert an identity neither subordinate to, nor dependent upon the authority of a male, Hammond aimed to 'contact a whole tradition of women's feelings', and to 'break down the distances between painting and sculpture, between art and "woman's work", and between art in craft and craft in art'.

In spite of the many positive facets of Chicago's endeavour, some questions soon arose. *The Dinner Party* was a huge project and Chicago did not work on it alone, requiring the collaboration of a number of helpers for its completion. The nature of her collaboration, that of a leader and amanuenses, was essentially no different to the kind of hierarchical structures which obtained throughout society. Despite her partial success in bringing the large number of women artists to the attention of the curators, collectors and critics responsible for deciding what would be shown and reviewed, what guarantees existed that such attention could be sustained? What was to stop those same curators, collectors and critics, after a decent interval, from finding further, equally 'valid' reasons for putting the works of art back in the basement again? Evidently it was not enough to promote women artists without at the same time working to dismantle the assumptions and institutional orthodoxies of the museum and gallery system, the collectors and the critics. In the years after the 'Great Goddesses' series, Mary Beth Edelson made a number of posters aimed at just such a subversion. In *Death of Patriarchy/A. I. R. Anatomy Lesson* (1976), for example, she took Rembrandt's *Anatomy Lesson* and collaged the heads of contemporary women artists onto the shoulders of the onlooking students, while transforming the cadaver from the body of an individual male into the corpse of patriarchy itself.

125

The wider implications of feminist thinking for art were becoming clearer by this time in the mid-1970s. Insisting on one's right to act as neither a neuter subject nor a surrogate male, but as a woman, had brought the issue of identity to the fore. Once recognized, it was, however, not an issue that could be contained within the debate on gender alone. Identity and an understanding of one's difference from the identities of others encompassed considerations of sexuality, social class and racial and cultural backgrounds.

Many artists who had already had some involvement with political issues in their work extended their analysis of these into the area of feminist consciousness. Adrian Piper (b. 1948) had begun her career as a hard line Conceptualist, but became increasingly aware of the degree to which her identity as a black woman affected the form and intent of her work. In her Performance work, she would adopt an androgynous, culturally ambiguous identity. With white face make-up, pencilled-on moustache, Afro hairstyle and mirrored shades, she would, as in *I Am the Locus #2* (1975), become a point of concentration for beliefs, attitudes and social forces. She stated: 'I am an anonymous third world young boy, wandering through the crowd, telling myself in an audible undertone that I am the locus of consciousness. ...I am both hostile to and removed from the presence of others.'

Also in the US, May Stevens (b. 1924) made a body of work centred on Rosa Luxemburg, the murdered German communist, and Martha Rosler explored *anorexia nervosa*, her *Losing: a conversation with the Parents* (1976) linking the condition not just to the question of female identity, but also to the role of the food industry in the larger play of economic and political forces which formulate our

100 May Stevens
Rosa from Prison 1977–80

notion of ideal beauty. Nancy Spero (b. 1926) made extended, scroll-
like panels containing drawings, fragments of text and repeated
imagery of a mythic nature. In *Torture of Women* (1976), for example,   101
the Babylonian legend of Marduk and Tiamat – in which Tiamat's
body is bisected to form the earth and the heavens – is laid alongside
the account of a Chilean model who was arrested and tortured by
General Pinochet's secret police.

Much work in Europe was expressly concerned with social issues
such as equal pay, child care, wages for housework and union representation for part-time working. All of these affected women
predominantly and connected with their more pervasive concern
to find a voice. As Lippard's comments on her own writing testify,
the problem extended right down to the basic tool of expression,
language itself. Even this, through its structure and the ideas attached
to words, contributed to the dominance of patriarchal attitudes. A
man, while speaking, could be himself. In contrast, a woman was
forced to utilize a language which, in a real sense, did not belong to
her, and could not be made to speak for her. In order to speak, she

99 (left) Adrian Piper *I Am the Locus #2* 1975

was always playing a part, or adopting a persona, or pretending to be something or someone she was not. If this were true of language, it was doubly true of the techniques of art. How could a woman paint without acknowledging the history of a medium in which her sex had played such a small part? Could traditional sculptural materials be separated from their inherent value within a market system founded upon equally traditional male-dominated power structures?

Even a cursory look at the history of painting would reveal the depiction of women as the object of men's desire. How, women began to ask, might it be possible for them to represent themselves in ways which would not automatically lead to their furtherance of that tradition? Just as separatism set up a distance from men for the purposes of organization and decision-making, so the use of new (or at least newer) materials and techniques pre-empted, to a certain extent, the problem of having to deal with the entire history of art before one could say anything new. Photography, video, film, sound, Performance – those information-providing tactics that had so recently begun to expand the bounds of art – all seemed more appropriate means with which to address this subject matter.

In the US, both Martha Wilson (b. 1947) and Jackie Apple (b. 1941) performed pieces in which they shifted identity and redefined themselves. Working together and with others in *Transformance: Claudia* (1973) they lunched, dressed for the part, in an uptown Manhattan hotel before descending in an aggressive and acquisitive posse upon the SoHo galleries. Eleanor Antin (b. 1935), too, made performances as, and constructed biographies for, a number of different personae. Although some of these – a prima ballerina, a nurse – accentuated accepted feminine qualities, others – a king, a black movie star – explored the question of who she was in unexpected ways. Antin said of these alter egos that 'the usual aids to self-definition – sex, age, talent, time, and space – are merely tyrannical limitations upon my freedom of choice'. In *Carving: A Traditional Sculpture* (1972), Antin photographed herself naked every day during a period in which she lost several pounds while dieting. Others in the US, including Laurie Anderson (b. 1947), Julia Heyward (b. 1949) and Joan Jonas (b. 1936) with her alter ego, Organic Honey, were involved in performance, sound and video work.

The split between the male-dominated public sphere and the conventionally pressured, 'contrasting', 'female' privacy of the home was undermined by work which embodied the feminist conviction that the personal *is* political. Instead of something which stifled

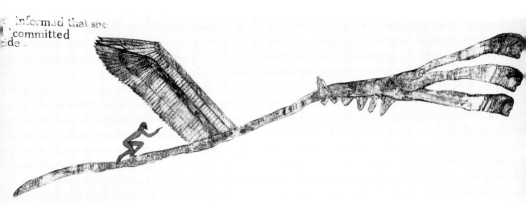

101 Nancy Spero *Torture of Women* 1976 (detail)

artistic activity, domestic life, reflected upon and transformed, became art's very subject matter. The 'Maintenance Art' series by Mierle Laderman Ukeles (b. 1939), begun in 1969, focused on the necessary functions of daily urban existence, particularly the disposal of waste and general cleanliness, usually ignored. One performance, *Touch Sanitation* (1979–80), involved her shaking hands with every employee of New York's sanitation department. In Britain, the performances of Bobby Baker (b. 1950) revolved around her inescapable responsibilities as a mother required to shop, cook and provide for her offspring. This focus on domestic reality, also present in the work of Tina Keane, Rose Finn-Kelcey (b. 1945), Kate Walker (b. 1938), Sally Potter, Rose English and many others, defied the conventional wisdom that certain types of subject matter were more important than others. During the late 1970s, Keane, rather than being limited by the responsibilities she had to her young daughter, instead exploited them, incorporating playground rhymes and children's games as content and structuring principle on a number of occasions. For the tape/slide work *Speaking in Tongues* (1977), Potter intercut a recording of herself addressing a crowd at Speakers' Corner in Hyde Park in London with a meditation on the character she had to adopt in order to be able to perform. Helen Chadwick (1953–96), a student in the early 1970s, began work using as her material her own body, its experiences, memories and potential and the

129

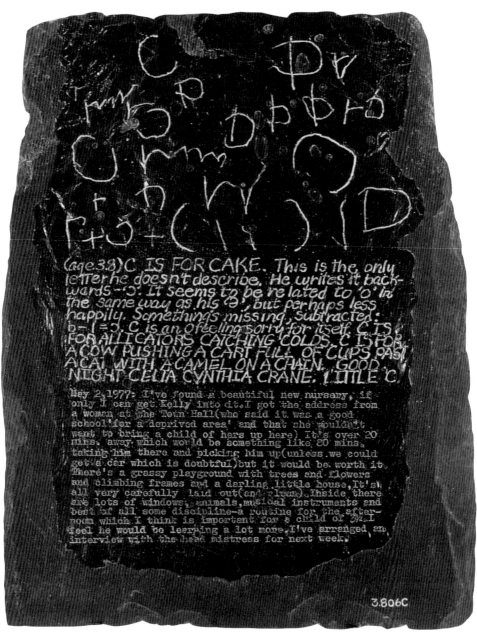

(age 3.8) C IS FOR CAKE. This is the only letter he doesn't describe. He writes it backwards-'Ɔ'. It seems to be related to 'o' in the same way as his 'Ɛ', but perhaps less happily. Something's missing, subtracted: b - I = Ɔ. C is an of eeling sorry for itself. C IS FOR ALLIGATORS CATCHING COLDS. C IS FOR A COW PUSHING A CART FULL OF CUPS PAST A CAT WITH A CAMEL ON A CHAIN. GOOD NIGHT CELIA CYNTHIA CRANE. LITTLE C.

May 2, 1977: I've found a beautiful new nursery, if only I can get Kelly into it. I got the address from a women at the Town Hall(who said it was a good school for a 'deprived area' and that she wouldn't want to bring a child of hers up here) It's over 20 mins. away which would be something like 80 mins. taking him there and picking him up(unless we could get a car which is doubtful)but it would be worth it. There's a grassy playground with trees and flowers and climbing frames and a darling little house, It's all very carefully laid out(and clean) Inside there are lots of windows, animals, musical instruments and best of all some discipline-a routine for the afternoon which I think is important for a child of 3½.I feel he would be learning a lot more, I've arranged an interview with the head mistress for next week.

3.806C

102 (above) Mary Kelly *Post Partum Document, Documentation VI* 1978–79

103 (right) Rebecca Horn *Unicorn* 1970–72

inescapable fact of its mortality. In all such work, the over-riding intention has been to make identity and personal experience reputable subject matter once again.

In 1975, the US artist Mary Kelly (b. 1941), then living in England, began her long-term project, *Post Partum Document*. The work's aim was to examine the process of socialization through which her newly born son was to pass during the first five years of his life. In order to do this Kelly collected and analysed the communications between her son and herself. In the first stage of the child's life, before his acquisition of any language, she was reliant on other signs to gauge his well-being, notably the state of his bowels as revealed by the contents of his nappies. These later gave way to words, drawings, sentences and more extensive, self-aware signals. Through this material, Kelly built up a picture of the process of entering into society and at the same time revealed how her participation in this process, as the child's mother, reinforced her own subordinate social position. Crucial to Kelly's thinking in carrying out this work was not only neo-Marxist theory, but also the structuralist reinterpretation of Freud carried out by the French psychoanalyst Jacques Lacan.

104 Susan Hiller *Dedicated to the Unknown Artists* 1972–76 (single panel, detail; installation, partial view; postcard)

The photographic, film and performance work of the German artists Ulrike Rosenbach, Katharina Sieverding (b. 1944) and Rebecca Horn (b. 1944) was concerned with personal and psychological, rather than overtly political aspects of identity. The artworks Horn made featured as props in her first films. Usually designed to be worn, they exaggerated or constrained some aspect of the body's

103   anatomy or function: by extending the head, as in *Unicorn* (1970–72) and on other occasions elongating the fingers, enclosing the body in feathers, or elaborately tying the legs and arms of two protagonists to each other so that independent movement became impossible.

Susan Hiller (b. 1942), another American living and working in Britain, had been trained as an anthropologist and continued to use something of the technique of fieldwork in her art. Collecting fragments of material culture – postcards, potsherds, newspaper clippings, wallpaper patterns – she incorporated these often cheap or trivial artefacts into installations that revealed and examined how they reflect and reinforce attitudes and beliefs within the society that

104   produced them. *Dedicated to the Unknown Artists* (1972–76) was begun when Hiller noticed that many towns on the British coastline sell postcards depicting rough sea conditions. She wrote, 'I treated the materials as keys to the unconscious side of our collective, cultural production. *Dedicated to the Unknown Artists* was about the contradictions between words and images, and dealt with the fact that words don't explain images – they exist in parallel universes.' Hiller's interest in the realm of dreams and the night led to a feminist appropriation of the Surrealist technique of automatic writing which, as 'fruitfully incoherent' writing, speech and song, has featured in many paintings and a number of sound and video installations since the 1970s.

A 1978 work of Hiller's, *Fragments*, recorded, arranged and interpreted Pueblo Indian potsherds. Each fragment of pottery formed a link, both real and imaginative, between Hiller's own culture and that from which it originated. This kind of connection, in which a mythologically rich ancestry breaks into contemporary reality, could also be found in the installations of Charles Simonds (b. 1945). Simonds fabricated miniature archaeological sites, ruins of some putative pre-Colombian civilization, and left them in the nooks and crannies of buildings in New York's Hispanic neighbourhoods. The critic Alan Moore wrote that his diminutive dwellings, 'provide a model of a civilization divorced from its context and remarried to another while at the same time they stamp the community with an imaginary underlife'. *Outside/Inside* (1974), as its name suggests, was

134

built either side of a shop-front window so that as time progressed the exterior portion disintegrated while the protected half remained pristine. This contrast between the fate of the two parts of Simonds's work highlights a dilemma for many artists in the 1970s. The thoroughgoing questioning of art and its institutions that had been accomplished in the preceding years would be of little value if the understanding it had revealed – of the importance of such things as environment, power, ownership, and cultural and sexual identity in determining what an artwork could mean – could not be put to some 'use'. The commercial gallery system was, of course, only one part of the larger capitalist market economy. There was inevitably conflict when art that expressed its rejection of that system was forced to rely upon it for its display, appreciation and consumption. Public art developed in part as a result of a desire to circumvent this dilemma. Using alternative locations such as shops, hospitals, libraries and the street itself as exhibition sites, and using the communication media – television, radio and advertising hoardings – as a more direct route to a broader, more egalitarian audience, public art turned its back on the galleries.

As feminism had argued with regard to work by women, just changing the venue was not enough. The method of working had to be reappraised as well. No longer was it acceptable for artists commissioned to make works for public places simply to impose their solutions upon a passive public. Lengthy periods of consultation, public meetings and discussion were entered into to establish the wishes and requirements of the local population before any work was undertaken. A working method such as that of Christo and Jeanne-Claude – who have never executed commissioned works and pay for all their projects themselves – could come into its own in such a climate. It has always been the case with their large temporary works of art, such as *Running Fence, California* (1972–76), *Valley Curtain, Colorado* (1970–72) and *Wrapped Coast, Little Bay, Australia* (1969), that the long period required to obtain the necessary permissions and permits and to organize resources and workers was as much a part of the work as the finished result.

Russian revolutionary art and the murals of the Mexicans Diego Rivera (1886–1957) and David Alfaro Siqueiros (1896–1974) were looked to as influential precursors by the public artists of the 1970s. The task of the mural was twofold: to depict events that celebrated the political power of the working class (in whose areas they overwhelmingly appeared) and to provide some visual excitement in

105

105 Christo and Jeanne-Claude *Wrapped Coast, Little Bay, Australia* 1969

what was otherwise usually a depressed and run-down area. Many of these community-based projects were completed across the US and Europe. To reject the gallery system on account of its inherent élitism would only be acceptable if the alternatives sought were a popular art rather than a populist one. If it were to appear in a public place this art should be acceptable to the majority and clear in its meaning, but should not simply pander to people. Consultation during the planning of the mural by Desmond Rochfort on the underside and supports of London's Westway, for instance, generated sufficient paperwork to constitute an exhibition display in its own right at the Serpentine Gallery's 'Art for Whom?' show in 1978.

Stephen Willats (b. 1943), who also showed in 'Art for Whom?', worked within well-defined, closed systems. Using the housing estates of west London as geographically distinct social units, he developed a series of questions through dialogue with some of the residents that the community at large was invited to answer. Collected answer sheets were then displayed for all to see how shared problems with health, noise, lack of leisure facilities, access, education, and so on, might be solved. *From a Coded World* (1976), *Vertical Living* (1978) and the *West London Social Resources Project* (1974), however, were not social work by another name. The works lasted for as long as it took to generate the questions and collect the answers. Any change that might be occasioned by the projects was not part of them.

In order to satisfy the criterion of general public acceptability, such work was often formally traditional and unambiguous in its meaning, displaying a strong sense of moral and educative purpose. One notable exception to public art's accommodation of figuration was the *Vietnam Veterans Memorial* (1982) in Washington D.C. by Maya Ying Lin. Here the restrained, radical abstraction of 1960s

106 Maya Ying Lin
Vietnam Veterans Memorial 1982

Minimalism, instead of being rejected as irrelevant to all but a privileged, specialist few, was embraced as particularly appropriate for a commemoration without celebration. An important phenomenon which rose to prominence at this time was graffiti art, which is discussed later.

Community-based work was no more free of economic constraints than the art from which it tried to distance itself. The difficulty of 'consuming' Performance, Installation and public art in the normal manner – buying them and taking them home – meant that they required subsidy funding in order to be able to exist at all. The 1970s witnessed a growth in public patronage. This was not a defeat of the art market, but a transfer of its operational imperatives into the field of national and local government. It is easy to be cynical and smile patronizingly at the misplaced idealism of those who thought that by making a direct appeal to the population as a whole they would convince many of art's value. But out-and-out cynicism would be misplaced, since the expansion of governmental and quasi-governmental involvement in funding of the arts was symptomatic of a growing belief in the necessity of art in a modern democratic society. Art was certainly not a luxury, but something that any self-respecting advanced society should expect as a mark of its civilized status. It might have seemed to some that receiving a grant from the National Endowment for the Arts in the US, or the Arts Council in Great Britain, or benefiting from state remuneration in Holland upon registering as a professional artist was little more than a sophisticated form of spongeing. A more enlightened interpretation was to recognize it as another responsibility of consensus politics. It was, however, no accident that this state of affairs obtained in the 1970s, precisely that period in which the postwar political consensus was playing itself out prior to the harder, fiscally deregulated realities of the 1980s.

An alternative funding strategy strove for self-sufficiency. In 1971, a group of artists, musicians and dancers including Gordon Matta-Clark (1943–78), Richard Landry (b. 1938), Tina Girouard (b. 1946) and Carol Goodden took over premises in New York's SoHo, refurbished them and opened the restaurant 'Food'. The old warehouses and light industrial buildings of lower Manhattan had been colonized by artists anxious to find cheap but spacious studio accommodation. 'Food' provided not only a service to this growing community, but also work, and therefore a means of financial support to many of its members.

107 Gordon Matta-Clark
Splitting 1974

Matta-Clark's next collaborative project, with some of his 'Food' colleagues but also with Richard Nonas (b. 1936) and Laurie Anderson, was 'Anarchitecture'. The group's aim was to focus on the gaps and undeveloped places within the urban environment: not the buildings so much as 'the places where you stop to tie your shoe-laces, places that are just interruptions in your daily movement'. This attitude was taken much further and to striking effect in the sequence of alterations Matta-Clark made to buildings between 1974 and his death in 1978. Cutting deep into their fabric – the first, *Splitting* (1974), involved slicing a house entirely in half – he practised what Dan Graham referred to as 'urban ecology'. He explained, 'His approach is not to build with expensive materials, but to make archi-tectural statements by removing in order to reveal existing, historical aspects of vernacular, ordinary buildings. Thus the capitalist exhaustion of marketable material in the name of progress is reversed.'

While some artists decided that the need for art with a social purpose required them to turn their backs on the galleries, this was by no means a universal conclusion. The norm remained, as with Land and Environmental art, that artists worked in a variety of locations and ways. In addition, of course, the gallery itself was ripe for investigation. Conceptual and post-Minimal practice provided the model for this. Michael Asher's spare installations made the gallery the object of contemplative attention, an 'object' that encompassed the historical, economic, administrative and other institutional dimensions to the built space. For an exhibition at Claire Copley's gallery in Los Angeles in 1973, he removed the dividing wall separating the showing space from the office, making the day-to-day running of the space, the arrangement of future exhibitions, the handling of sales enquiries and the work of publicity into a display. In 1979, invited to make a work for the permanent collection of Chicago's Museum of Contemporary Art, Asher designated a portion of the building's exterior cladding as the 'work'. While on display, the cladding was removed from the façade and hung on an interior wall. The curatorial decision to exhibit it was therefore not idle, but one that affected the very body of the institution. The

108, 109 Exterior and interior views of the Museum of Contemporary Art, Chicago with Michael Asher's work installed, 1979

museum was, quite literally, shaped by its exhibitions policy. Once its period of display was over, the artwork was put into storage and removed from sight by being replaced on the museum's frontage.

Painting by no means disappeared during the 1970s, although the impact of the new theoretical framework within which art was being produced forced its thoroughgoing critical re-evaluation. For some, enamoured of the critical radicalism of Conceptualism, painting stood, in Victor Burgin's phrase, as 'the anachronistic daubing of woven fabrics with coloured mud'. In this light, though, Conceptualism could only be the academically approved opposition to modernism. If it had something to offer, it was an opening-up of technical and practical possibilities, not a set of aesthetic prescriptions that merely substituted one set of materials and techniques for another. Political or Social art, with its interest in the relationship between the realms of aesthetics and politics, broadened the perspective of this otherwise bland dichotomy. In the 1960s, for followers of

Clement Greenberg, the refusal to represent distanced art from sordid reality, while for Michael Fried's so-called 'literalists' the stamp of 'objecthood' made it a part of reality. Thus, in painting, what in the 1960s had been an argument over the interpretation of abstraction, was transformed in the 1970s into a debate about the apparent significance and political connotations of figurative or non-figurative work.

By the end of the 1970s, Art & Language had begun to work on a series of 'Portraits of Lenin in the Style of Jackson Pollock'. The marriage between the quintessentially abstract and the symbol of Socialist Realism – heroic representation subordinated to the political will of the state – would appear to be impossible; as impossible, in fact, as the social realities they represent, the ideological and cultural programmes of capitalism and communism, finding some accommodation between themselves. Yet because, rather than in spite of, this paradox, the paintings work. Pollock's drip technique, perhaps the most individual painterly signature of the century, proves to be easily reproducible and out of its skeins – which seem arbitrary but which must in this instance, of course, be very deliberately placed – drift the familiar features of the father of the Russian revolution. The paintings are both abstract and representational and yet all their elements can be seen to represent something. This understanding that all things connote meaning, whether they happen to resemble something else or not, made art appear to be political whether or not it chose to present itself as such. To eschew political commitment as being outside the proper responsibility of aesthetics, as some painters and sculptors chose to do, could therefore be easily condemned as reactionary because of its furtherance of the traditional, formalist approach to art.

In 1975, Rosalind Krauss and Annette Michelson, two contributing editors of *Artforum*, left the magazine to found a new journal, *October*. The journal was named 'in celebration of that moment in our century when revolutionary practice, theoretical enquiry and artistic innovation were joined in a manner exemplary and unique'. The crude Socialist Realist argument, that a political cause was furthered by its sympathetic representation, was rejected. The editorial of the first issue of *October* proclaimed: 'Art begins and ends with a recognition of its conventions. We will not contribute to that social critique which, swamped by its own disingenuousness, gives credence to such an object of repression as a mural about the war in Vietnam, painted by a white liberal resident in New York, a war

110 Art & Language *V. I. Lenin by V. Charangovitch (1970) in the Style of Jackson Pollock II* 1980

fought for the most part by ghetto residents commanded by elements drawn from the southern lower-middle-class.'

The desire expressed by the editors of *October* for in-depth theo-retical debate across disciplines was symptomatic of the growing acceptance that something really had changed in art. While Pop and Minimalism and their various aftershocks could still be described as responses to, and therefore as part of, late modernism, the kind of 'intertextuality' being propounded here was of a different nature. Beuys's Free International University maintained an avowed revolutionary intent by holding on to the idea that it was possible to imagine a wholly different set of social circumstances and orient oneself towards achieving them. *October*'s intertextuality, drawing on the neo-Marxism of the 1960s revolts, the psychoanalytic analysis of subjectivity and identity in feminism and the phenomenological tradition explored by Minimalism (most fruitfully apparent in the writing of the French philosopher Jacques Derrida whose influence, by the mid-1970s, had transformed critical discourse) was the web of an encompassing and inescapable social reality. The artist was as much a prisoner of this reality – or, at least, the theoretical descriptions of this reality – as anyone else, and the realization of this fact meant that the notion of art as a reflection upon the conditions of the world made from a safe critical distance was now untenable.

Modernism had, in the words of the English historian Perry Anderson, three interrelated elements: a strong sense of the historical progress of the economic, political and social spheres, an academic *status quo* against which to work and the fruits of considerable technological advance. The first, the idea of progress, was less credible in the wake of successive wars, the repressiveness of communism and the growing realization that an advance for the West was often the opposite for some other part of the world. Equally, in the field of ideas, the recognition that research, far from being innocent enquiry, was almost entirely dictated by economic and political circumstances external to its object undermined the thought that the growth of knowledge was in any way directed towards some larger enlightenment. People usually derived knowledge from needing information either to help them build better weapons, or to enable them to patch up those wounded by them more effectively. Lastly, the enquiring character of contemporary art, with its proliferating range of materials and forms, had long ceased to value novelty for its own sake as a potential weapon, if indeed it ever had. Art's diversity, even in its radical, 'political' forms, became now the academic and institutional norm. The accommodation of public art, artist placement and Performance by state and regional funding bodies was mirrored in education, where colleges expanded their curricula to offer courses not only in painting and sculpture, but also in mural design and other catch-all 'disciplines' such as combined, alternative, or experimental media. Modernism, at least as it had been understood and described from Manet and the Impressionists onward, had, it was thought, reached its terminus; we were now to see the world as postmodern. Utopia had been replaced by dystopia.

CHAPTER FOUR

Postmodernisms

Financial deregulation had as great an impact on art as on everything else, and in the 1980s the dealers came back into their own. In 1981, the German-based curator Christos Joachimedes wrote: 'The artists' studios are full of paint pots again.' The remark introduced the exhibition, 'A New Spirit in Painting', held at the Royal Academy in London, and curated by Joachimedes together with Norman Rosenthal of the Royal Academy and Nicholas Serota, then Director of the Whitechapel Art Gallery and subsequently of the Tate. The following year, the Italian critic Achille Bonito Oliva coined the term 'International Trans-avantgarde' as the title of his book proclaiming the re-emergence of painting to pre-eminence in the art world. He wrote: 'The dematerialisation of the work and the impersonality of execution which characterised the art of the seventies, along strictly Duchampian lines, are being overcome by the re-establishment of manual skill through a pleasure of execution which brings the tradition of painting back into art.'

Oliva stressed the passing away of the idea of progress in art. There was no longer one, linear 'story of art', but a multiplicity of attitudes and approaches jostling for attention. One of the consequences of art being released from step-by-step development was a freedom to look anywhere for inspiration: instead of the struggle to develop a current style by carrying forward and responding to the character of the immediately preceding one, Trans-avantgarde art could, or indeed should, quote from any period it liked. Furthermore, it need not now restrict itself to fine or 'high' art but could equally well adopt craft and other 'low' cultural techniques, materials and subject matter where appropriate. Newness could no longer be a criterion of judgment because newness or originality, it was realized, were unattainable, if not downright fraudulent. Everything had already been done; all that remained was for us to take fragments of what was to hand and combine and recombine them in ways that were meaningful. A postmodern culture was one, therefore, of quotation, and viewed the world as a simulacrum. Quotation could appear in a number of guises – as copying, pastiche, ironic reference, imitation, duplication, and so on – but however striking its effect, it could make no claim to originality. These guises, however, covered a wide spectrum of critical positions. There was undoubtedly an element of nostalgia in the Trans-avantgarde or, as it was widely termed, neo-Expressionism. Count Giuseppe Panza di Biumo, one of the most important collectors of Minimal and post-Minimal art, regarded it as a move backwards rather than forwards, a regression to an art that was easily appreciated after the apparent difficulty of much 1960s and 1970s art. To promote the latest art as essentially a return to painting, particularly the kind of large format, macho gestural painting that had been challenged by feminism, was a marketing exercise, a conservative rejection of Conceptualism's critical enquiry and a capitulation to the insistent demands of the market.

There was also a side to postmodernism that relished the unseemliness of an art that made itself by borrowing. Juxtaposing disparate styles and images from different sources did violence to the intentions behind, and the historical integrity of, the original. What could one make, say, of Markus Lüpertz (b. 1941) painting Germany's past as a Surrealist landscape in a pseudo-Expressionistic way: *The Triumph of Line III, 'Monument with Burned Bones'* (1979)? The unease felt by some at this behaviour led to charges that postmodernism was, simply, devoid of any sense of history, that its products were cynically cobbled together from elements seized because of their superficial visual appeal and that it was therefore itself only an art of surface, lacking substance. In contrast to the negativity of these positions, described by the American critic Hal Foster as 'a postmodernism of reaction', there was also a critical, radical postmodernism. Far from the collapse of the idea of progress leading to a situation of 'anything goes', in which all gestures and interpretations had equal validity, it was possible, having absorbed the lessons of the previous two decades, to question the assumptions behind and meanings of art's borrowings.

As Oliva's book recounts, and as 'A New Spirit in Painting' and *Zeitgeist* – a subsequent exhibition in Berlin also selected by Joachimedes and Rosenthal – showed, painting was again ·in the limelight. Notable exponents at this time were: in Italy, Francesco Clemente (b. 1952), Enzo Cucchi (b. 1949), Sandro Chia (b. 1946) and Mimmo Paladino (b. 1948); in Spain, Miquel Barceló (b. 1957) and Ferrán Garcia Sevilla (b. 1949); in France, Gérard Garouste (b. 1946), Jean-Michel Alberola (b. 1953), Jean-Charles Blais

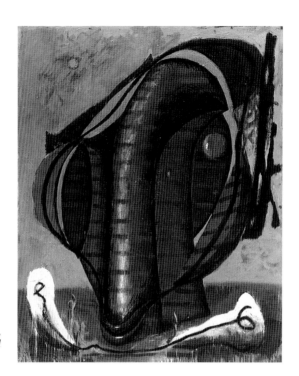

111 Markus Lüpertz
*The Triumph of Line III,
'Monument with Burned
Bones'* 1979

(b. 1956), Robert Combas (b. 1957); in Britain, Christopher LeBrun (b. 1951), Paula Rego (b. 1935), Bruce McLean; in Germany, Anselm Kiefer (b. 1945), Georg Baselitz (born George Kern 1938), Markus Lüpertz, Gerhard Richter; in the US, Julian Schnabel (b. 1951), David Salle (b. 1952), Eric Fischl (b. 1948), Jack Goldstein (b. 1945); in Denmark, Per Kirkeby (b. 1938); in Holland, René Daniëls (b. 1950); and in Belgium, Narcisse Tordoir (b. 1954). There is no sense in which these artists together constituted any kind of movement – their work was far too varied in appearance and intention for that to be the case, and anyway, postmodernism's pluralism prohibited anything as coherent as a movement – but as much as anything, it was this huge variety that allowed Oliva to bracket them together.

In Italy, Clemente's work was strongly autobiographical, combining images in a rhythmic and free-wheeling way that implied an erotically charged atmosphere without quite suggesting a narrative. One image leads to another and then another, without ever turning out towards the world. Clemente worked in a number of different media, but kept their use segregated according to the country in

which he worked. Large paintings in oil on canvas, as in *The Fourteen Stations* sequence (1981–82), were executed in New York. Chia's subject matter played in a tongue-in-cheek manner with the fear of not living up to expectations. His overburdened *Water Bearer* (1981) asks how a young artist, working in Italy, a country with such an illustrious cultural heritage, could hope to match the grandeur of past achievement he saw all around him. Cucchi's energetically worked surfaces drew their imagery from themselves, envisaging the act of painting as a continuing process of making, rather than a fixing of representations on canvas. Mimmo Paladino's paintings and his later multi-part sculptural installations disposed figures and props with symbolic and mythic resonance within dramatically depicted spaces. These artists and others – Nicola de Maria (b. 1954), Nino Longobardi (b. 1953), Bruno Ceccobelli (b. 1952), Gianni Dessi (b. 1955) – appeared alongside the older Arte Povera figures Mario Merz, Jannis Kounellis and Pier Paolo Calzolari, rather than supplanting them as the new generation.

148

In Germany, the imagery of many painters concerned the causes and consequences of postwar division. This was not a new pre-occupation, and the predominant figures of the early 1980s, far from being young unknowns, were artists who had been working for some time: Gerhard Richter and Sigmar Polke from the 1960s and Georg Baselitz, Markus Lüpertz, Jörg Immendorff, Bernd Koberling (b. 1938), Dieter Hacker and K. H. Hödicke (b. 1938) right through-out the 1970s. There was also, in Germany, less of a sense that paint-ing needed to reassert itself. In much of this work clear evidence of the stylistic influence of Expressionism could be seen, and it was generally referred to as neo-Expressionism. Ernst Ludwig Kirchner's work and primitivism were reworked by Helmut Middendorf (b. 1953), and emerged in the febrile sexuality of Rainer Fetting (b. 1949) and Salome (b. 1954), these three being dubbed the Neue Wilde. In the case of Baselitz, Expressionist influence lay in his han-dling of paint and his acknowledged debt to, and direct quotation from, Nolde. Baselitz, born in East Germany, had painted pioneers from early in his career. Battle-scarred, tattered, and becoming frag-mented as the political tutelage of his youth was reconsidered, his work had nevertheless retained a breezy heroicism. In 1967 his work underwent a literal revolution: in *Finger Painting I – Eagle – à la* (1971–72), he painted his subject matter upside down. To paint

112 (left) Francesco Clemente
The Fourteen Stations, No. III
1981–82

113 (right) Georg Baselitz
Finger Painting I – Eagle – à la
1971–72

abstractly was too nebulous a proposition for Baselitz. He needed an image of some sort to provide a rationale for the laying on of paint, but at the same time did not wish the recognition of that image to obscure an appreciation of the brushwork and colours of the painting itself. Painting upside down – which is to say actually painting upside down, not painting the right way up and turning the finished canvas through 180 degrees – was his solution to this problem. The image was there as an ordering principle for the pigment, but that pigment was able to have its full impact before the image was recognized.

As Hölderlin and Nietzsche had done in the nineteenth century, Kiefer examined critically the mythic and historical dimensions of the German sense of identity and nationhood. More explicitly than most, he focused on the period of Nazism and the Second World War. The 'scorched earth' paintings of 1974, such as *Maikäfer Flieg*, depicted landscapes blackened either by stubble burning or the depredations of war. The transforming power of fire was repeatedly used by Kiefer as a metaphor for the artistic process. Straw, too, was used as an ironic symbol of the same: a reference to Rumpelstiltskin who span straw into gold. Ironic questions abound. The stairs up to an early studio feature: are they the ascent to a place of spiritual grace? Similarly an artist's palette makes frequent appearances, some-times with wings: is the vain hope of transcendence held out by art an adequate substitute for lost religious faith? Another studio, a disused brickworks bought in the late 1980s, is pictured again and again in countless manipulated photographs. The photographs are bound, sometimes in huge books with pages of lead. Too heavy for a single human to lift, they lie open on a lectern or are housed in gar-gantuan shelving units. Kiefer used straw again in a major series of 1981 entitled, after the refrain in the Jewish poet Paul Celan's *Todesfuge*, 'Your golden hair Margarethe/Your ashen hair Sulamith', a reference to the victims of the Holocaust. One or other of the lines is scrawled across each canvas, charging landscape or figure with emblematic significance.

In a different way, Lüpertz's paintings also dealt with myth and reality in German history. He adopted the Nietzschean term 'dithyramb' – Dionysian song – as a generic title. Immendorff con-tinued to make paintings with strong political content. If his work also looked stylistically to earlier German art, it leant towards Neue Sachlichkeit rather than Expressionism. The 'Café Deutschland' series, begun in 1977 and continued in the early 1980s, presented the realities of a divided Germany in bar scenarios. By the later 1980s, as

114 (right)
Jörg Immendorff
Eigenlob stinkt nicht 1983

115 (below)
Gerhard Richter
18, Oktober 1977 c. 1988

in *Nachtmantel* (1987), the inhabitants of Immendorff's restaurant and theatre interiors had become the denizens of the art world. His one-time associate and fellow artist A. R. Penck (b. 1939), his teacher Beuys, his colleagues Lüpertz and Baselitz, the art dealers Michael Werner from Cologne and Mary Boone from New York, the American artists Schnabel, Salle and Fischl, the European curators Rudi Fuchs and Joachimedes and many more curators, artists, collectors and critics all engaged in the niceties of the social dance.

Richter's output included both abstract and representational paintings, although his method of working meant that it was never easy to say where the dividing line between the two fell. The figurative canvases were always copied from reproductions, photographs, postcards or media images, never from 'real life'. A late-1970s series of abstract canvases, for example, were in fact faithful enlargements made from slides of small oil studies. In 1988, he returned to source material he

116 (above) Anselm Kiefer
Margarethe 1981

117 (left) Eric Fischl
Bad Boy 1981

118 (above right) Julian Schnabel
Oar: for the one who comes out to know fear 1981

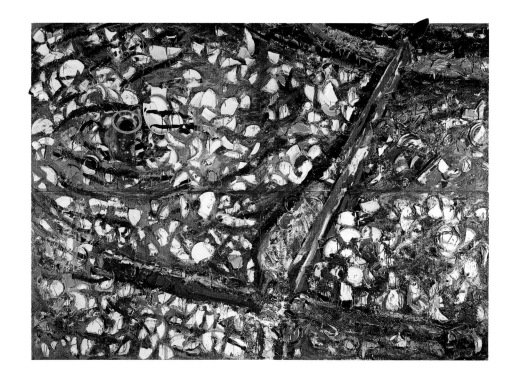

had kept for over a decade, an exhaustive collection of images documenting the prison suicides of the members of the Baader-Meinhof terrorist group. Wary of possible charges of sensationalism, Richter stipulated that the resultant sequence of grey paintings, collectively titled *18, Oktober 1977*, were only to be shown together.

115

Polke's use of imagery and media was a paradigm of the eclectic nature of 1980s art. His work had a notable influence outside Germany on the painting of Julian Schnabel, whose characteristic early-1980s style was to paint a similarly varied range of imagery – from high art to advertisements and cartoons – on a ground of broken crockery. The paintings, usually large and necessarily bulky in order to support the weight of the ceramics, were spectacular in effect, their forms animated by their fractured surfaces. Subject matter was of a piece with this spectacle: a female crucified Christ in *Vita* (1983), for example, and, on an old piece of haulage lorry tarpaulin covered in grime and bootprints, a bravura blue shape entitled *Portrait of God* (1981). Schnabel's sense of the significance of materials was one he saw himself sharing with both Polke and Kiefer, something that all three ultimately derived from Beuys's example. He wrote: 'A lot of Americans still don't understand that it was Beuys who instigated this current shift in art. They think it came from reductivism and minimalism and painting being dead and then resurrected – but I'm talking about an involvement with materials. ...Even if the materials are manufactured, or they look new, the work has to do with the alchemic and accumulative power of...objects.'

Also in the US, David Salle's paintings fitted more neatly into the notion known as 'appropriation' that was widespread in the early 1980s. Appropriation, the opportune seizing of things for our own use, was the activity to which we were all sentenced by our condition of postmodernity. The flat areas of colour in *The Trucks Bring Things* (1984), or *How to Use Words as a Powerful Aphrodisiac* (1982), on which floats a mixture of material culled from many sources, were clear examples of this. Salle's frequent use of soft-porn imagery was read as an example of a feminist backlash. Eric Fischl did not so much appropriate as consciously refer to the style of Max Beckmann in his psychological portrayals of leisured existence, such as the deck full of naked figures in *The Old Man's Boat and the Old Man's Dog* (1982) and the pubescent sexuality of *Bad Boy* (1981).

The US and Germany were the two poles of the art world in the 1980s, with New York and Cologne as their most important centres. The Cologne dealers had inaugurated a Kunstmarkt (art market) in 1967. Düsseldorf, Cologne's near neighbour, started one five years later. The two alternated thereafter until 1983, by which time the Cologne Art Fair had established itself, along with the more traditional event in Basle, as one of the prime displays of artists' wares in the calendar. There were others of longer or shorter pedigree in Paris, Chicago, Milan and elsewhere. One was set up in the late 1980s, just before the end of the economic boom, in Frankfurt, and another, ARCO in Madrid, enjoyed a period of success in the latter half of the decade as a result of the socialist government's generous arts funding policy.

ARCO was, in fact, just one factor in the much greater international visibility which art from Spain enjoyed from this time onwards. The sculptors Susana Solano (b. 1946), Juan Muñoz (b. 1953) and Cristina Iglesias (b. 1956), and the painter Federico Guzmán (b. 1964) were among those who became more widely known. Muñoz's installations had a theatrical air and were peopled by caricatured and exaggerated figures: dwarfs, puppets and isolated body fragments. In line with his interest in de Maria, Guzmán's

154

119 Susana Solano *Thermal Station, No. 1* 1987

painting/objects, which often extended out from a flat surface into the room containing them, played on the unresolvable relationship between representation and occupying a space. Although very different in look and feel, Iglesias's wall-mounted structures similarly evoked aspects of architectural experience through a mode of visual address appropriate to painting. Solano's welded metal works emphasized the importance of Spain's re-entry into the art world since they reconnected the experimental developments in art since the 1960s to the strong Iberian strand in modernism. A sculpture such as *Thermal Station, No. 1* (1987), for example, as the American critic Kim Bradley has noted, certainly acknowledges the direct simplicity of Minimalism, yet its materials and formal allusiveness also place it in a line of sculptural descent from Picasso and Julio Gonzalez through Eduardo Chillida (b. 1924).

In the new deregulated economic circumstances, the business of collecting exerted an enormous influence on art. The new Museum of Contemporary Art, for example, opened in Los Angeles in 1983 with a show of works drawn from eight large private collections including those of Count Giuseppe Panza di Biumo and Peter Ludwig (Haacke's 'Chocolate Master'). Other lenders included Charles and Doris Saatchi, whose collection was founded on the success of the advertising agency Saatchi ran with his brother, Maurice. Chosen mainly by Doris Saatchi to begin with, the works represented at the Saatchi Museum, which opened in 1984, included those of Judd, Warhol, Serra, Flavin, Chamberlain and Andre and provided solid grounding for a rapidly expanding stock of new art. In 1985, a four-volume catalogue of the collection was published under the definitive title, *Art of Our Time*. The Saatchi Museum was a converted paint factory in north London and was used as a venue for temporary exhibitions of works selected from the collection. The consequences of the growth in art buying were predictable. As with any other commodity, the restricted supply resulted in an increase in value; new prices would quickly be confirmed, if not improved upon, by purchases from the contemporary sales at the major auction houses. The renewed interest in painting had profound implications for this booming market. An individual's manual skill was reinstated as proof of an object's artistic credentials, and this meant that, instead

120 Malcolm Morley *SS Amsterdam in Front of Rotterdam* 1966

121 Howard Hodgkin *In Bed in Venice* 1984–88

of being merely analysed as if it were a commodity, art could now properly function as one. Aesthetic pleasure could be marketed just like soap powder and coffee beans.

Embracing the idea that art could and should be publicized, an annual award, the Turner Prize, was instigated by the Tate Gallery in 1984. Initially sponsored by the New York financial institution Drexel Burnham Lambert, the Turner Prize survived their bankruptcy at the end of the 1980s boom, and still provides contemporary art with a prominent public forum. The US-based English artist, Malcolm Morley (b. 1931), whose photographically accurate paintings of ocean liners had been prominent in the late-1960s Hyper Realist movement, was its first recipient. His 'Day of the Locust'

series of the late 1970s, while done in a looser style than hitherto,
included direct references to earlier, tightly controlled works, particularly *SS Amsterdam in Front of Rotterdam* (1966). Morley's example
demonstrates that as well as bringing forward the work of many
younger artists, the renewed interest in painting also brought back
into new focus the careers of an older generation. Barnett Newman
and Mark Rothko had both died in 1970, but of the Abstract
Expressionists both Willem de Kooning and Philip Guston (1913–80)
were still alive and making new work. Guston had, in fact, ceased to
paint in his earlier lyrical abstract style and had begun to portray
himself, as in *The Studio* (1969), as a cowled presence amid the
doubts and difficulties of the working environment. Graphic evoca-
tions of the Classical civilizations by Cy Twombly (b. 1929) – *Hero
and Leander* (1981–84), *Anabasis* (1983) – were only the most recent
in a career that stretched back to his Abstract Expressionist roots in
the 1950s; from Minimalism there were Agnes Martin (b. 1912),
Robert Ryman and Brice Marden (b. 1938).

In Britain, the biggest contribution from older generation artists
was from Howard Hodgkin (b. 1932), Francis Bacon (1909–92),

122 Philip Guston
The Studio 1969

123 Leon Kossoff
Christchurch Spitalfields,
Morning 1990

R. B. Kitaj, Michael Andrews (1928–95) and the painters of the 'School of London', i.e. those artists who were associated with the painterly representational approach of David Bomberg: Frank Auerbach (b. 1931) and Leon Kossoff (b. 1926). There was no shared style in the work of this group: the thickly worked and dribbled paint of Kossoff's *Christchurch Spitalfields, Morning* (1990), like that of his portraits, is a long way from the flat, colourful strokes of Hodgkin's *In Bed in Venice* (1984–88).

The market even found a way to bring some parts of public art back into its orbit. The burgeoning in the US of urban graffiti into large-scale, colourful tableaux was recognized as a vivid art form. Using not only walls, but also mobile sites such as railway carriages which took the work from the city to the suburbs and beyond, graffiti art quickly became a pervasive presence throughout the US and Europe. The opportunism of practitioners who used any conveniently available blank surface to spray complex paintings of exuberant expressiveness – provocative DIY murals of greater urgency and immediacy of impact than the polite, democratic products of bona fide community arts projects – was in tune with the newly vitalized market. The tactic, quite simply, was to offer the sprayers – or, at least, those who had higher ambitions – a surface inside a gallery to paint rather than an exterior wall.

Wary of the exploitation that could occur in such circumstances, Tim Rollins (b. 1955) collaborated with youngsters drawn largely from within the poorer Puerto Rican population of New York who were keen to work creatively, but who, because of circumstances, had had little formal training. Rollins and K. O. S. (Kids of Survival), using literature as a starting point, read a text and discussed imagery that might be appropriate to it. This was then sometimes painted over a canvas on which the pages of the original book had been pasted. In other cases, images were drawn onto the pages of books. The project was educative as well as artistic, growing from the after-hours group 'Art and Knowledge' Rollins had set up in the school where he taught. Texts studied and used in more than one work included Herman Melville's *Moby-Dick*, Lewis Carroll's *Alice in Wonderland* and Franz Kafka's *Amerika*. The presence of text, the grid effect of the rows of pages underlying what was often predominantly monochromatic painting, and the shared authorship of the works was, for Rollins, a natural development of his background in the political discussions of New York Conceptualism. All participants, however, were adamant about distancing their working pattern from the exploitative relationship that existed between the art world and graffiti. As Rollins said, 'We learned a lot from the situation of what happened to graffiti artists, and how a white audience can treat that work: embrace it with such enthusiasm, and then get rid of it the next year with equal enthusiasm. Particularly with black and Hispanic artists, that tends to be the pattern.'

For Kenny Scharf (b. 1958), Keith Haring (1958–90) and Jean-Michel Basquiat (1960–88) it was the style of graffiti that was put to expressive purpose in their work. Basquiat came to notice as 'SAMO', whose tag, in a well-conceived campaign of self-promotion, appeared on walls outside all the best art-world venues. His paintings were full of words and phrases that had been crossed out, altered and substituted for better versions. Far from signalling nonchalance or thoughtlessness, this pervasive editing represented a struggle to clarify and to communicate. He said, 'I just look at the words I like, and copy them over and over again, or use diagrams. I like to have information, rather than just have a brush stroke. Just to have these words to put in these feelings underneath, you know.'

124 Tim Rollins and K. O. S. *Amerika VI* 1986–87

Cumulatively, Basquiat's paintings conduct a harsh critique of contemporary America and of the position of black people within it: 'Black people are never portrayed realistically, not even portrayed, in modern art, and I'm glad to do that,' he said. *Discography two* of 1983 125 copies, with deliberate repetitions, emphases and crossings-out, the liner notes for a Bebop LP onto a square, black canvas: the archetypal modernist image, that has already travelled from Malevich to Reinhardt and beyond, is here invested with new significance and sent off in another direction. In 1980, Basquiat stopped using his 'SAMO' tag; he was taken on by the Annina Nosei gallery in New York and given materials and a basement space to work in. Four years later he was with one of the major and most glamorous New York galleries of the 1980s, owned by Mary Boone, and able to sell his paintings for $100,000 apiece. The year after that saw a collaboration with Warhol and an appearance on the cover of the *New York Times* Sunday colour supplement sitting barefoot in his studio wearing an Armani suit. And two years after that he was dead, overdosed, a victim of his indulgence in the rewards of the demeaning patronage he had so despised.

Keith Haring's outlined humans and animals cavorted in Day-Glo splendour. They began in the very early 1980s as chalk drawings on 126 black paper pasted over expired posters on subway billboards; his work always retained that connection. He could show paintings and sculptures at the New York galleries of Leo Castelli or Tony Shafrazi, but the instant demotic appeal of his cartoon, stick-figure style meant that it worked equally well on T-shirts, badges, stickers and

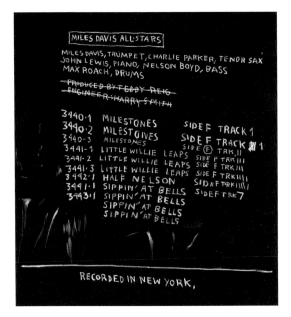

125 Jean-Michel Basquiat
Discography two 1983

posters. The 'Pop Shop', which he opened in New York in 1986, sold merchandise bearing his designs, but he would also design for fund-raising and advertising campaigns, particularly those associated with AIDS, of which he died in 1990.

The impact of AIDS on the art world in New York was profound. Act-Up, the organization of artists fighting among other things to promote AIDS awareness and the interests of those who were HIV positive, staged events and demonstrations. The impact of AIDS was clear, too, in the kind of work that drew on 1970s art with a social 128 purpose for its formal and expressive means. The group Gran Fury made informative, educational and forthrightly propagandistic posters, magazine spreads and exhibition displays. On one occasion they mimicked a United Colors of Benetton campaign in a bus advertisement attacking indifference and prejudice. Bureaucratic 129 indifference is also the subject of *Arena* (1992) by Frank Moore (b. 1953), one of the magical realist canvases which communicate his fury at and sensitivity to AIDS; figures are depicted in the midst of nightmarish medical procedures, toxic waste and chemical pollution. No less direct were the writings and images of David Wojnarowicz (1954–92). 'I'm a blank spot in a hectic civilisation', he wrote in *Memories That Smell Like Gasoline*, published in 1992, the year of his

126 Keith Haring *Untitled* 1983

death from AIDS: 'I'm a dark smudge in the air that dissipates without notice. I feel like a window, maybe a broken window.' The *Sex Series* of photomontages (1988–89) used negative imagery from numerous sources to assert, in the face of society's response to AIDS, that 'I will continue to explore my body and the bodies of other men and find the possibilities for pleasure and connection'.

Concern with AIDS is visible in less obvious ways in the abstract painting of the early and mid-1980s. In 1981, Ross Bleckner (b. 1949) exhibited paintings at the Mary Boone gallery, some of which, like his *Growing Grass* of 1982, copied the illusionistic abstractions of Op art. Two years later, Philip Taaffe (b. 1955) did the same with

127

127 David Wojnarowicz *Sex Series* 1988–89

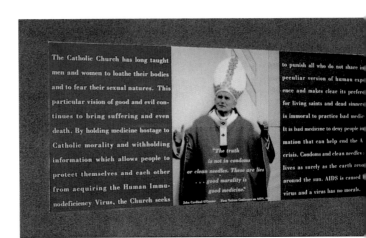

128 Gran Fury *Untitled* 1990 (partial view)

129 Frank Moore *Arena* 1992

paintings whose richly decorative surfaces were built up from printed paper pasted onto the canvas. The undulating black-and-white stripes of *Overtone* (1983) were the most obvious reprise of Bridget Riley's earlier work. Shortly thereafter, Peter Schuyff (b. 1958) made some work strongly reminiscent of another Op artist, Victor Vasarely. Considering the general political and economic situation as well as the advent of AIDS – a phenomenon he likened elsewhere to the plague, a medieval visitation at the heart of the late twentieth century – Ross Bleckner suggested in 1987 that 'people in their early 20s are now thinking about death more'. The use of Op by these artists was a way of dealing with this. Coming as it had at the very end of the modernist trajectory, Op stood as the most played-out, most empty, non-referential, non-art of the entire century. Using this as an 'image' of hopelessness, a hopelessness defied by their continuing to make paintings rather than to capitulate and give up altogether, these artists were able to do in a way what art had always done: to project beyond the present moment. Bleckner's particular quality of light, Taaffe's use of ornament as a means to relieve unremitting circumstance and Schuyff's 'spotlit' grids that might be skin blemished by Kaposi's sarcoma each reintroduce utopia to dystopian reality.

Ashley Bickerton (b. 1959) worked in a similar way. His elaborate, box-like, wall-mounted metal units covered in abstract fragments, logos, symbols and stylized lettering, made a display of the method and logic of their construction. They were described by him in suitably bleak terms: 'I'm just kicking the great big, corpulent, cellulitic body of art as it lays there in its deathbed, and creating a sort of perverse poetry out of the whole thing, I guess.' This is a long way from modernism. The startling power of Malevich's *Black Square* in 1913, the dynamic balance and primary-coloured rhythms of Mondrian's pre-Second World War 'Neo-plasticist' compositions and even the concern with abstraction of Caro, Kelly, Stella and Olitski in the 1960s rested in some degree on the belief that it was possible to make art that was non-representational. By the 1980s, in both chronological and practical terms, painting was post-Conceptual. The compound styles and joky titles – *Blobscape* (1986), *The Big Picture* (1988) – of the American Jonathan Lasker (b. 1948), and the Day-Glo renditions by another American, Peter Halley (b. 1953), of Newman-inspired designs showed that they could use the history of abstraction as a painterly vocabulary. Their work sat comfortably alongside that of an older generation: not only Richter, but also, for

130 Philip Taaffe *Overtone* 1983

example, Olivier Mosset whose abstraction, like that of his early
associates Toroni and Buren, was always Conceptual, and Richard
Artschwager (b. 1923), whose 1960s work had bridged Pop and
Minimalism. The geometrical simplicity, usually rectilinear, of
Mosset, Halley, Meyer Vaisman (b. 1960), the Swiss John Armleder
(b 1948), the Austrians Helmut Federle (b. 1944) and Gerwald
Rockenschaub (b. 1952), among others, was nicknamed neo Geo.
Not quite new, only neo-, this latest manifestation of abstract painting was taken to be a copy or simulation of the real thing. Halley
dubbed the large Day-Glo blocks of colour and connecting black
lines in his paintings cells and conduits: *Yellow and Black Cells and
Conduit* (1985), *White Cell with Conduit* (1986), and so on. These
spaces and their interlinkings mapped out the systems of contemporary exchange. Less an agglomeration of private and public
territories, our social space was now a collection of nodes within the

132

131 Ashley Bickerton *Le Art (Composition with Logos 2)* 1987

132 Peter Halley *White Cell with Conduit* 1986

networks of communication. Halley was greatly influenced in his work by the theories of Jean Baudrillard, whose ideas on 'hyper reality' described a world in which images no longer represented a real object, but referred the viewer to another image, then another, in an endless sequence. It was a world in which simulation was not the pretence of a 'real experience', but was itself the only kind of reality we could ever hope for. The loss of originality meant that everything was a copy, and, without an original, the idea of copying with its pejorative overtones made no sense anyway. By making paintings that replicated those of Picasso, on the other hand, the approach of Mike Bidlo (b. 1953), made perfect sense in a world where advertisements stole from other advertisements, where music pirated snatches from other songs, where films spoofed other films and the lives of characters were prolonged through perpetually extendable series and where the invasiveness and ubiquity of TV

133 Robert Gober
Untitled 1991

erased the boundaries between public and private and between fact and fantasy.

As previously noted, the term widely used to describe the copying of already existing images by Taaffe, Bidlo, Sherrie Levine (b. 1947), Elaine Sturtevant (b. 1926), Jack Goldstein and others was 'appropriation'. For the American art historian Thomas Crow, such imitation was made possible by the fact that 'the authority of art as a category' had ceased to be the matter of contention that it had been throughout the modernist period: 'In narrowing artistic mimesis to the realm of already existing signs, these artists simply accept, with a serene kind of confidence, the distinction between what the modern cultural economy defines as art and what it doesn't.'

Postmodern theories that described contemporary culture as one of surfaces and images had a particular appeal in Australia, a country largely 'Western' in its perceptions but geographically quite isolated. Because of that isolation, many artists' understanding of contemporary art was gleaned far more from illustrations in magazines than from seeing the real thing. Imants Tillers (b. 1950) worked with this circumstance, making paintings entirely put together from the images of Baselitz, Kiefer and Schnabel amongst others. His paintings were, moreover, done on many small art board panels rather than a single, large canvas with the result that works could be more easily parcelled up for shipment out of the country to an exhibition venue elsewhere. As an ultimate appropriation of the appropriationists, Tillers's *Double Covenant* (1987), made for his first exhibition in New York, borrows Philip Taaffe's *We Are Not Afraid* (1985), an image of defiance and hope, which is itself derived from Barnett Newman's 1960s 'Who's Afraid of Red, Yellow and Blue' series, which is a return to the primary directness of late Mondrian after the poetic tonalities of Abstract Expressionism.

Robert Gober (b. 1954) noted on this point that the US 'in particular is nurtured on and transfused with images of duplicity'. His plaster sinks, while referring to Duchamp's readymade *Fountain* were, like all his work, made by hand. Gober's installations also evoke an ambivalent sexuality, as, occasionally, had some of Duchamp's work. In rooms wallpapered with a forest scene, a penis and vagina motif or a hanged man and sleeping boy pattern, Gober variously placed his sinks, convincingly genuine boxes of rat bait and cat litter, wax limbs with protruding candles and inset plug-holes, a hand-sewn wedding dress, bundles of newspaper in which the top story had been mocked up to highlight intolerance and social repression, and a hugely oversized cigar.

39

133

170

134 Robert Gober
Double Sink 1984

The work of Jeff Koons (b. 1955) and Haim Steinbach (b. 1944) was, along with that of Gober and Bickerton, considered to be object-making of a neo-Conceptual kind. Steinbach collected shop-bought products displayed on formica-covered shelf units. Although often quite different kinds of things were placed together, their colours, materials, textures and shapes made the arrangements coherent in the way that an individual's lifestyle is shaped by his or her particular choices from among the variety of mass-produced goods available. Steinbach's shelves, with titles like *dramatic yet neutral* (1984) and *related and different* (1985), reflected the growing acceptance that while we might all be consuming the same commodities, the way in which each of us does so is quite distinct. Koons's interest in the acceptance of commercial products as art, his employment of skilled workers to make his work for him and his concentration on the infamous – not least himself – as subjects, all marked him out, for some, as the natural successor to Warhol. The displays of upright and wet/dry vacuum cleaners in spotless, fluorescent-lit perspex cases he began in 1980 are perhaps another homage to Duchamp. Bulbous containers, long floppy tubes, rigid upright forms and the tension between dirt and pristine purity rework the Dadaist's eroticism and his admiration for American plumbing as the country's one great artwork for a new era. In the mid-1980s, a number of stainless steel casts of a plastic inflatable bunny and a Bourbon decanter shaped like the train on the Jim Beam Bourbon label among other things, reaffirmed the distance between the usefulness of ordinary artefacts and the reflective value of art. The Jim Beam decanter remained art

135

135 (left) Haim Steinbach
related and different 1985

136 (right) Jeff Koons
*One Ball Total Equilibrium
Tank* 1985

only so long as the seals and the Bourbon it contained were intact. *One Ball Total Equilibrium Tank* (1985) can be seen as the pared-down expression of art's striving towards perfection and the ideal. A sealed glass tank containing a basketball sits on top of a metal stand. The balance between the weight of the ball and the density of the salt solution surrounding it allows the ball to rest at the exact centre of the container. It is a beautiful illusion – look, no strings, the gravity-defying feat of the body in slow-motion replay as it soars towards the hoop – all the more so because nothing is hidden.

This attitude was what the German critic Wolfgang Max Faust called 'the paradox of an "unbelievable belief" in art'. The same paradox was evident in the work of some Cologne-based artists of the generation after Kiefer. Albert (b. 1954) and Markus Oehlen (b. 1956), Werner Büttner (b. 1954), Georg Herold (b. 1947), Martin Kippenberger (b. 1953), Walter Dahn (b. 1954) and Georg Jiri Dokoupil (b. 1954) belonged to this generation. Both Polke and Immendorff had taught many of them, and another important

influence on them was the Danish Situationist Asger Jorn. Dokoupil, who changed style for each new batch of work, was, with Dahn and Peter Bömmels (b. 1951), a member of the Mulheimer Freiheit group of neo-Expressionists. Albert Oehlen and Kippenberger used the Expressionism of the moment to question the orthodoxies it seemed to be reintroducing. Paintings such as Kippenberger's jumble of angular forms titled *With the Best Intentions I Can't Find a Swastika* (1984) and Oehlen's Kiefer-aping imagery or his study in red, yellow and blue called *Portrait of A. Hitler* (1985) parade a cynicism towards the oppressive rectitude of liberal thinking. Herold's sculptures looked like knocked-up affairs, although the wire and underpants of *Egypt* (1985) from the 'German Speaking Summit' series, the bricks and tights of *Hologram* (1986) and the cheap wood and cardboard of his constructions, as well as the brief, cryptic words they bear, have a resonance carried over from Beuys and Polke.

Some of the sculptural objects by Rosemarie Trockel (b. 1952), such as *Komaland* (1988) with its tights stretched by organically inspired plaster forms, had a similar feel to Herold's, with the addition of an awkward sensuousness. As well as these, there was a series of large knitted paintings and wearable garments. Tiny wool marks, hammers and sickles, swastikas or the words 'West Germany' covered jumpers and balaclavas or made up expansive monochrome fields. Another wool 'painting', *Cogito, Ergo Sum* (1988), had Descartes's dictum across a mainly white surface. It is a post-feminist assertion of female identity, but the area of black in the bottom right hand corner also echoes Polke's 1969 painting, *Higher Powers Command: Paint the Upper Right Corner Black!* The early sculptures of Katharina Fritsch (b. 1956) excited wonder and controversy in equal measure. The

137 Martin Kippenberger
*With the Best Intentions
I Can't Find a Swastika* 1984

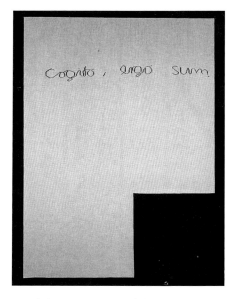

Höhere Wesen befahlen: rechte obere Ecke schwarz
malen!

138 (left) Rosemarie Trockel *Cogito, Ergo Sum* 1988

139 (right) Sigmar Polke *Higher Powers Command: Paint the Upper Right Corner Black!*
1969

crowd-pulling 1987 *Elephant* was a full-size green plastic model, cast
from a specimen at the Bonn Natural History Museum, and placed
on a tall, oval plinth. Fritsch's interest in making copies appeared
more explicitly in *Tischgesellschaft* (*Company at Table*) evoking society's   142
fear of technological advance. Cloned figures sit on either side of a
long table, their identical hands resting on a cloth patterned with a
computer-generated design.

140 Andreas Gursky
Tokyo 1990

141 (above) Candida Höfer
Natural History Museum, London II
1990

142 (right) Katharina Fritsch
Tischgesellschaft 1988

143 Louise Lawler *How Many Pictures* 1989

The 1980s also saw the emergence in Germany of a substantial group of artist photographers – Thomas Ruff (b. 1958), Thomas Struth (b. 1954), Andreas Gursky (b. 1955) and Candida Höfer (b. 1944) – all of whom had been pupils of Bernhard and Hilla Becher. Ruff made large portraits of his contemporaries in the art world and, with the same typological approach, catalogued the southern sky at night; Struth recorded black-and-white cityscapes, remarkable for their lack of human inhabitants, and made studies in the world's major museums of people looking at art. Höfer photographed educational and cultural institutions as a means of representing the values embodied within them, while Gursky's large scenes of activity that are often shot from above – as in the electronics factory, *Karlsruhe* (1991), and the busy stock exchange

144 (left) Sherrie Levine *Untitled (After Walker Evans #3 1936)* 1981

145 (right) Jenny Holzer 'Truism' on T-shirt modelled by Lady Pink 1983

140 floor, *Tokyo* (1990) – demand to be viewed almost as paintings. The Canadian Jeff Wall (b. 1946) self-consciously displayed his use of the conventions of photography in setting up his large, back-lit cibachrome images. Wall had participated in Conceptualism in the late 1960s, and a 1980s work such as the sweatshop confrontation *The Outburst* (1989), made in that critical spirit, was precisely composed and rehearsed in order to make viewers conscious of the stereotypes they rely upon and the cultural assumptions they make when reading an image.

The feminism of the 1970s appeared in the changed conditions of the next decade in work by Sherrie Levine, Cindy Sherman (b. 1954), Louise Lawler (b. 1947), Barbara Kruger (b. 1945) and Jenny Holzer (b. 1950) that looked critically at the issues of consumption. Levine confronted the power of the male gaze and its presumption of possession, folding it back on itself by paying attention to the products of male creativity. Copying works by Kandinsky, Feininger and others and presenting them as her own

146 (right) Cindy Sherman *Untitled Film Still* 1977

(because they were her own) she suggested that the question of originality could not be separated from a consideration of who was allowed to be original. The point was perhaps most clearly made in Levine's photographs 'after' Walker Evans and Edward Weston, retakes of images by two of the pioneers of American photography, of which the American critic Craig Owens wrote: '[Is] she simply dramatising the diminished possibilities for creativity in an image-saturated culture, as is often repeated? Or is her refusal of authorship not in fact a refusal of the role of creator as "father" of his work, of the paternal rights assigned to the author by law?'

In the spirit of Asher and Broodthaers, Lawler conducted a renewed examination of the ways in which art attains value as it finds its place in the system of exchange and display. *How Many Pictures* (1989), for example, shows, through the reflection of a Frank Stella painting in a gallery's highly polished floor, how indissolubly linked are work and context. Kruger adopted the techniques of display design in her photo-texts. Stark messages in bold white out of red sit over black-and-white images: *We won't play nature to your culture* (1983), *Your gaze hits the side of my face* (1981) and other pronouncements of similar intent questioned the relations of power within our commodity culture.

Sherman's 'Untitled Film Stills' of the late 1970s and early 1980s are, as are almost all of her subsequent works, self-portraits. Endlessly

mutable, she appears again and again in different situations. The studied stylistic coherence of each black-and-white photograph makes it resemble a still, around which one could easily dream up a filmic narrative complete with plot and characterization. The lie to one's instinctive grasp of Sherman's identity in these pictures is given by the next in the series, and the next, which each present her as an entirely different person. After the 'Film Stills' and another series in which she parodied glamorous magazine poses, her work became somewhat darker featuring monstrous bodies, decay and rotting food shot in rich colour. With her so-called 'vomit pictures' Sherman asked whether it would be possible to take a picture that could overcome the appeal of the medium and be unhangable. Inevitably, the seductive appeal of the medium itself meant that the answer was no. In later work, the characters she adopted, both male and female, were drawn from old master paintings. Here, as much as in the earlier series, Sherman's desire was not so much to become these characters as to efface her own self, becoming blank in a manner reminiscent of Warhol.

145 Holzer's 'Truisms', short statements with a strong impact but an ambiguous meaning were fly-posted, stuck up in telephone booths and printed on T-shirts: 'Protect me from what I want', 'Lack of charisma can be fatal.' As the decade progressed, she moved into more officially sanctioned public communication sites, putting her art on illuminated advertising boards in places such as Times Square or Piccadilly Circus. Although her work has been shown to great effect in galleries, most notably at the Guggenheim Museum in 1989 and in Venice the following year where she was the first woman to represent the US, it is in the public arena that they have had most impact.

The Polish-Canadian Krzysztof Wodiczko (b. 1943) co-opted the power and symbolism of public buildings and monuments for his work. Using projectors with tungsten lamps, he treated their façades as screens on which to project images that provided an ironic commentary on their meanings: US and Soviet missiles chained together over the arch of the Soldiers and Sailors Memorial Arch in Brooklyn (1984), a small swastika on the pediment of the South African embassy in Trafalgar Square, London (1987) and Ronald Reagan's hand as he took the oath of allegiance on New York's AT&T building during the 1984 presidential campaign. These, like Holzer's, were temporary displays, gestures that activated an environment without imposing upon it unduly.

147 Richard Serra
Tilted Arc 1981

Public art in the 1980s was considerably removed from its 1970s beginnings. In the US and Europe, agencies specializing in public art became established as the territory became more and more a part of the development boom. Where building projects required the inclusion of works of art such agencies would oversee the selection and commissioning of an appropriate artist. 'Percent for Art' schemes were also widely introduced, whereby one percent of the total cost of any development had to be earmarked for expenditure on art. Elsewhere, a developer like Sir Stuart Lipton, responsible for

London's Broadgate Centre, could, as a collector, decide which of his own works he wished to place around the site. Richard Serra, whose *Fulcrum* (1987) stands at one of the entrances to Broadgate, had been making sculpture for many years that was, in the increasingly popular phrase, site-specific. This meant that what the sculpture was, where it was placed and how it might produce its effect were inextricably linked. Moving such a work even a short distance would result not just in a re-siting, but in the creation of an altogether different sculpture.

The tensions that still existed between the general public and art, ostensibly conceived with the public's well-being uppermost in mind, were amply demonstrated in the argument over and ultimate fate of Serra's *Tilted Arc*, commissioned under the US art-in-architecture scheme in 1981 for New York's Federal Plaza. The steel sculpture – much taller than human height – cut across the plaza, severely restricting the view and progress of pedestrians. By 1985, protest by those who worked in the surrounding buildings had reached such a pitch that the General Services Administration, the government body that had commissioned the work, stated that it should be moved. A court case ensued, with Serra maintaining that its removal would constitute a violation of his contract and that a proposed relocation to one side of the plaza was of no use, as the work had been conceived for its original position. Any alteration to that would effectively destroy the work. It was eventually removed in 1989.

While some aspects of public art maintained the separation between the culture of the gallery and the demotic wholesomeness of emancipation from it, there were many more artists whose practice spanned both gallery and public site. Curatorial projects brought this to the fore. In 1986, the Belgian Jan Hoet organized *Chambres d'Amis*, a large-scale project in Ghent that was both public and private. More than forty families submitted parts of their homes to an artist for the duration of the exhibition. The viewer, therefore, had to take a map of all the locations and spend several days moving around the town knocking on doors and ringing bells in order to see the whole show.

In spite of the size of the exhibition, no artists from Britain were invited to participate. Hoet's explanation for this omission was that British artists were more involved in making objects than in the investigation of space and temporality. The artists to whom he was referring were a group of sculptors, many of whom emerged from the Royal College of Art in the mid- to late 1970s: Richard Deacon

148 Richard Deacon
Art for Other People No. 10
1984

(b. 1949), Tony Cragg (b. 1949), Antony Gormley (b. 1950), Bill Woodrow (b. 1948), Shirazeh Houshiary (b. 1955), Anish Kapoor (b. 1954), Alison Wilding (b. 1948) and Richard Wentworth (b. 1947). Deacon's sculptures in laminated wood, riveted metal, rubber and plastic combined allusions to both engineered and biomorphic forms, as can be seen in the tongue-in-cheek echoes of everyday objects in his long sequence of small-scale works, the 'Art for Other People' series. Lead casts of his own body, Gormley's sculptures relate the figure and its dimensions to the space around it. Both Cragg and Woodrow used discarded material. Woodrow snipped and folded the casings of consumer durables into new shapes that speak of spectacle, excitement, danger and the media's treatment of these: the side of a twin tub turns into a guitar, the panel of a car door becomes a gun and a microphone, and the seat of a child's tricycle folds into a tank. At the beginning of the 1980s, Cragg was

149 Reinhard Mucha
*The Figure-Ground Problem
in Baroque Architecture* 1985

collecting discarded items in wood or plastic and making arrangements of them on the floor. Exemplary of the approach and of Cragg's position in a sculptural tradition is *New Stones – Newton's Tones* (1978), a rectangular array of plastic fragments arranged *à la* Long and graded to form a spectrum of colour.

In Germany, Reinhard Mucha (b. 1950) and Meuser (b. 1947) were also both recycling the discarded remains of an industrial past. Meuser's compositions of plates and girders left each element as it was, thereby using the 'found colour' in which they were originally painted. Their titles, too, provided a sign of their origin and former function: *Metro Station Overkampf*, or *Krupp* (both 1987), for example. Mucha's sculpture was centred on the construction sites, steelworks and extensive railway network around his Düsseldorf home. A large-scale work such as *The Figure-Ground Problem in Baroque Architecture* (1985), made for the Centre Georges Pompidou in Paris, uses equipment and materials found in the museum itself. Other works incorporate scavenged items, especially old doors, within finely crafted and elaborate framing structures. Mucha's work is autobiographical, rooted in its place of origin, and often makes use of elements from previous works in a continuing recreation of the past: personal, social and artistic.

149

150 Tony Cragg *New Stones – Newton's Tones* 1978

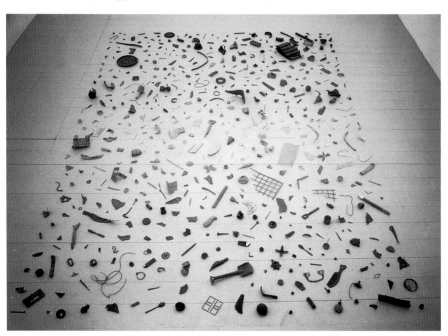

CHAPTER FIVE

Assimilations

Andy Warhol died at the beginning of 1987. His presence had been a profound influence for a quarter of a century. The photo-portrait of him by Richard Avedon (b. 1923) showing his bullet scars, taken following Valerie Solanas's unsuccessful assassination attempt the day after Bobby Kennedy was killed in 1968, made him, as the American critic Lisa Liebmann wrote, seem immortal. 'How can he be so right?!' the US art critic Peter Schjeldahl remembered thinking, 'with mingled awe and fury. He even got shot at the historically correct moment, if such is conceivable.' Two days before he died, the 32 Campbell's Soup can paintings that made up his first show at Irving Blum's Los Angeles gallery – all of which Blum had bought and kept together – went on permanent loan to the National Gallery in Washington. In the light of this, the news of his death seemed for Liebmann to presage something catastrophic. She wrote: 'On the morning of Sunday, February 22 with the news that Andy Warhol was dead, I ran to the window expecting to hear seismic noises coming from the city outside, and to witness a transfiguration, I don't know of what: of the back of the building facing me, of the air quality, of appearances in general – but of something. The shock of so enormous an absence would surely register, it seemed, on reality itself.' The shock of his passing was, however, no more than equal to the impact of his emergence, as the artist Larry Bell wrote on first seeing Warhol's work in 1963: 'Warhol has successfully been able to remove the artist's touch from the art. He has not tried to make a science out of it as Seurat did, but made an anti-science, anti-aesthetic, anti-"artistic" art totally devoid of all considerations that we may have thought of as necessary. He has taken a super-sophisticated attitude and made it art, and made the paintings an expression of complete boredom for aesthetics as we know it. ...It is absolute, it is painting, most of all it is art. In any event, and no matter what is finally decided about it, nothing can take away from it the important changes that the work itself has made in the considerations of other artists.'

151 Judith Barry *Echo* 1986

Two years after Warhol's death, in 1989, the Los Angeles Museum of Contemporary Art staged 'Forest of Signs', an exhibition named after a line in Baudelaire's poem 'Correspondences' that brought together many American neo-Conceptual artists including Koons, Steinbach, Lawler, Levine, Sherman, Judith Barry (b. 1949) and Barbara Bloom (b. 1951). Barry's *Echo* (1986) investigated the conflict between the liberating promise of modernist architecture and the dehumanizing effect of so much contemporary glass and steel-frame urban design. Bloom contributed an installation entitled *The Reign of Narcissism* (1988–89), a mock Neoclassical interior in which all busts, wall reliefs, moulding details and vitrine-encased objects bore her silhouette or likeness. 'Forest of Signs' was subtitled by its curator, Mary Jane Jacob, 'Art in the Age of Reagan'. As the painter and critic Jeremy Gilbert-Rolfe (b. 1945) suggested in a lecture given during the exhibition, a better description might have been 'Art in the Age of Andy'. The only European figure of equivalent stature to Warhol throughout this period was Joseph Beuys, and he had died the year before Warhol. These two deaths coincided with a change of circumstance and perception that accompanied the absorption of the lessons of the previous quarter century's experimentation. The

popularity of Installation, the maturity of video work, the transformed strategies of public art and the continued relevance of work
that specifically addressed the social issues of oppression, racism and
sexuality can each be witnessed in several of the major exhibitions
since then.

The apogee of generalized postmodern creative practice that
sought to draw parallels between various forms was Documenta VIII
in 1987. A large work by Beuys in the main museum's central space
acted as a poignant focus for the proceedings. The theme of the
Documenta was art and design, and designers and architects were
included among the exhibitors along with artists. Ettore Sottsass
(b. 1917), Jasper Morrison (b. 1959), Paolo Deganello (b. 1940),
Hans Hollein (b. 1934), Haus Rucker Co. (Laurids Ortner (b. 1941),
Günter Zamp-Kelp (b. 1941) and Manfred Ortner (b. 1943)), Arata
Isozaki (b. 1931) and others bore witness to the fact that many facets
of these disciplines had apparently converged. Among the exhibits,
the entry of the Iranian-American Siah Armajani (b. 1939) was a
design for a footbridge to be installed in the sculpture garden outside
the Walker Art Center, Minneapolis, and the construction of the
German Thomas Schütte (b. 1954) was a pavilion selling ice cream
and drinks, complete with WC. Ange Leccia (b. 1952), a Corsican,

152 Barbara Bloom *The Reign of Narcissism* 1988–89

presented one of the latest Mercedes Benz cars on a revolving pedestal.

Leccia's 'Arrangements' of manufactured items – anything from Concorde aeroplanes down to radio-cassettes – are one example of art in which the act of display is a central concern. It is central not because it separates the commodity as artwork from its appearance in everyday life, but because it reproduces it. When Warhol showed his Brillo and Campbell's Soup boxes back in 1964, they were, for all the shocking banality of verisimilitude, artful copies. He used wooden boxes, in effect Minimal sculptures, onto which were pasted silk-screened logos to make them look like the real thing. Leccia used the real boxes. Similarly, *Poison* (1992) by the Swiss Sylvie Fleury (b. 1961) heaps together the smart designer carrier bags from her shopping trips complete with their contents, and the 1986 exhibition at the Cologne Kunstverein of the Belgian Guillaume Bijl (b. 1946) turned the gallery into a functioning menswear store. At first sight, works such as these resemble those of Steinbach and Koons, but there is little irony in them. Rather than using the reflexive criticality of Conceptualism to frame their practice, these artists take its lessons as read.

In 1986, Rebecca Horn, Jannis Kounellis and the German playwright Heiner Müller proposed the staging of an exhibition in Berlin which would include two works by each participant, one to be shown on either side of the Wall. By the time the project was realized in 1990 as *Die Endlichkeit der Freiheit* ('The Finitude of Freedom'), the Wall had come down and the process of unification was under way. The artists had to adjust to this new reality. *The Missing House* (1990) by Christian Boltanski (b. 1944) was sited in the gap made in a terrace in the former Jewish quarter of East Berlin by

155

153 (left) Sylvie Fleury
Poison 1992

154 (right) Hans Haacke
Die Freiheit wird jetzt einfach gesponsert – aus der Portokasse (Freedom is now just going to be sponsored – out of petty-cash) 1990

155 Christian Boltanski
The Missing House 1990

an Allied bomb in 1945. Fixed to the exterior walls of the houses to either side of the space were the names and dates of occupation of former residents. Further detailed documentation was displayed at the now derelict exhibition area that had once housed El Lissitzky's *Proun Room* at the 1923 Grosse Berliner Kunstausstellung. For his 154 contribution, Hans Haacke used one of the observation towers still standing in the Potsdamerplatz. Once the central point of Northern Europe, the square had been cut in two by the Wall and was now cleared and whole again prior to being redeveloped. Haacke placed the Mercedes Benz logo, symbolic of the corporate muscle that would dominate the reshaping of the city, on top of the tower, and to one of its sides fixed Goethe's words 'Kunst bleibt Kunst' ('Art remains art'). In both cases, the public nature of the work was able to engage with the historical, political and economic dimensions of the urban context without compromising its artistic qualities.

190

156 Rachel Whiteread
House 1993

'The Finitude of Freedom' was symptomatic of the way in which public art, when it was not merely an adjunct to or an aspect of urban planning, had overwhelmingly come to be conceived as a series of temporary interventions. The British agency Artangel commissioned several such short-term projects in the 1990s, notable among which were *Work for the North Sea* (1993) by Bethan Huws (b. 1961) and *House* (1993) by Rachel Whiteread (b. 1963). Huws invited the Bulgarian singers, Bistritsa Babi, to sing by the water's edge on a Northumberland beach at high tide on a summer's evening. The 'work' was a coming together of their singing, Huws's choice of time and location, and the unpredictable contributions of the prevailing sea and weather conditions. Whiteread's *House* was a cast of the interior space of a house in east London. The last of a terrace to be demolished to make way for a park, the building's solitary presence stood as a brief monument, a focus for much strong

191

feeling about London's homeless and a trigger for memories of other, long-forgotten dwelling places.

Despite, or perhaps because of, the impending financial strain of German unification and the likelihood that the seat of power – at that time in nearby Bonn – would move to Berlin taking much money and cultural activity with it, the mood in Cologne in 1990 was determinedly bullish. Nine dealers in the city pooled their resources and their artists to mount a single group exhibition, 'The Köln Show', that spread throughout their respective venues. 'Nachschub', proclaimed the front cover of the catalogue: supplies, back-up, reinforcements. The military overtones were still there, despite thirty years during which art had undermined the idea of an avant-garde allied to historical progress. It was, nonetheless, an apt tag for those in the show and for some American artists closely associated with them in attitude and spirit: for the performances and videos of Andrea Fraser (b. 1965), in which she acted as a gallery guide; for the investigative analyses and installations of Fareed Armaly (b. 1957) and Mark Dion (b. 1961); the proposals of Peter Fend (b. 1950) for remodelling the earth for sound political, economic and ecological reasons; the laconic and witty wall drawings of Jessica Diamond (b. 1957); and the investigations of sexuality and prejudice by Zoë Leonard (b. 1961) and Larry Johnson (b. 1959). Armaly's *Orphée 1990*, at the Maison de la Culture, Saint Etienne that year, recreated the design and décor of the building at its opening in the 1960s as part of André Malraux's drive to provide access to culture for all. Dion's elaborate laboratory-cum-attic installation, *Frankenstein in the Age of Biotechnology* (1991), infused the prospect of genetic research with an excitement akin to the 'Boy's Own' adventuring of nineteenth-century exploration. These and many others of the sixty artists could be seen as working in ways established by Broodthaers, Haacke, Asher, Smithson, Nauman and Mary Kelly. Diamond's *Yes Bruce Nauman* (1989) explicitly acknowledged the debt to that artist.

In his catalogue essay, Diedrich Diederichsen looked at the fears that the changes in global power relations had unleashed. 'The misery of being exploited', he said, quoting the musician and writer Mayo Thompson, 'is nothing when compared to the misery of not even being exploited any more.' In looking at the art being made in these new circumstances he suggested new criteria of judgment: 'Pornographic is the adjective that ought to replace the pejorative "decorative" in art criticism. It is a term for work that takes no responsibility for its origin. Trash, in contrast, takes all responsibility.'

157 Mike Kelley *Dialogue #2 (Transparent White Glass / Transparent Black Glass)* 1991

Trash and an unimpeachable sense of failure were everywhere present in the performances, videos, objects and installations of Mike Kelley (b. 1954). 'Why I became a performance artist', says one piece showing photographs of naked young women. A series of banners made in 1987 in the colourful style of those designed by the former nun Mary Corita Kent, hold remorselessly nerdish messages: 'I am useless to the culture but God loves me', 'Pants shitter and proud. P. S. Jerk off too (and I wear glasses).' Kelley has often used home-made soft toys, playthings invested with inordinate amounts of love and care with their intended recipients in mind, which, in the dirt of their old age and abandonment, speak of unbearable dereliction and loss. His 'Arenas' and 'Dialogues' of the late 1980s and early 1990s, arrangements of toys scattered on and under knitted blankets, treat this issue of abandonment in formal terms derived from the critical, yet still positive, language of Minimal and post-Minimal sculpture. The 'slacker'-like dysfunctional anomie of Karen Kilimnik (b. 1962), Jack Pierson (b. 1960), Raymond Pettibon (b. 1957) and Sean Landers (b. 1962) ploughs a closely related furrow. Kilimnik's

193

158 Simon Patterson *The Great Bear* 1992

installations such as *Mrs Peel...We're Needed* (1992) map the action
fantasies of bedroom-bound, TV-addicted youth, while her *faux-naïf*
texts *Jane Creep*, about an eponymous imaginary friend, hint that it
will not take much to tip the mental balance over into psychosis:
'JANE'S BEST FRIEND IS MAKING A JANE DOLL + STICKING PINS IN IT.'

In Britain some of the most interesting art of the late 1980s and
early 1990s was associated with London's Goldsmiths' College. Julian
Opie (b. 1958) and Lisa Milroy (b. 1959) had studied there earlier in
the decade. Milroy, in the earlier part of her career, painted things to
buy – shoes, shirts, coats and hats – singly or in neat rows. Larger
canvases of plates, potsherds, tyres or lightbulbs, relied on the abstract
order of the grid to bring cohesion, a sense of a complete picture, to
the collected elements. Some, such as *Lightbulbs* (1988), had the feel
of a trade catalogue impassively offering a huge variety of goods to
cater for all requirements, except that they were lovingly painted in

oils. Opie's sheet metal sculptures from 1983 were painted to mock their own eminent saleability: a cheque-book and pen, five supermarket items, five old masters. Conversely, the next series were abstract forms given titles of socio-political import lifted from newspaper headlines. The work subsequently drew more obviously on Minimal form by parading an absence of function in its likeness to chill cabinets, ventilation ducts and office partitions that stressed the primacy of the visual in art. Milroy and Opie were exhibiting internationally within a very short space of time, and provided a model for those who followed.

While still a Goldsmiths' student in 1988, Damien Hirst (b. 1965) obtained the use of a disused building from the Docklands Development Corporation, and, within its generous spaces, put on 'Freeze', an exhibition that included many of his fellow students. Collectively, they were in tune with the entrepreneurial spirit of the times, and their enterprise in setting up the show and, perhaps more

159 Damien Hirst
I Wanna Be Me
1990–91

significantly, persuading several important dealers and curators to travel out to see it, paid off. The exhibition was quickly followed by others of a similar nature – such as 'Modern Medicine' in 1990, also co-curated by Damien Hirst – whose participants also supplied the clutch of new private galleries in London owned by non-British dealers. Among those who appeared via this route were Anya Gallaccio (b. 1963), Angela Bulloch (b. 1966), Simon Patterson (b. 1967) and Gary Hume (b. 1962). Gallaccio's installations involve perishable or mutable materials such as flowers, fruit, ice or chocolate arranged and then left over a period of days or weeks to decay and change as circumstances dictate. *Stroke* (1993) saw the Karsten Schubert Gallery painted with chocolate: 'chocolate box' art with faecal overtones. Visitors licked the walls for a little pleasure if they had the nerve. Bulloch's works in light, sound and other media are sometimes activated randomly, but are more often triggered by the presence of a viewer, as with the drawing machine, *Blue Horizons* (1990). Another series that collected together rules of conduct posted up in various places – topless bars, hotels and offices – emphasized the universality of the need for human acquiescence if society is to be run smoothly. Patterson finds in names, both famous and unknown, the means to examine value, historical perspective, educational priorities and personal characteristics. *The Great Bear* (1992) replaced the station names on the London Underground map with lists of footballers, comedians, philosophers, newscasters and others to make a quite different but no less readable map of contemporary cultural space. The dimensions of Hume's early gloss-painted abstract works and their placement of circular and rectangular areas of relief were derived from the porthole windows, finger- and kick-plates of hospital doors. He subsequently used figurative motifs which were important as much for formal as for narrative reasons. Hirst's medicine cabinets were *fin de siècle* wall sculptures *à la* Don Judd, stuffed with the artificial means necessary to achieve the desired goal: *New York* (1989), or *I Wanna Be Me* (1990–91). His pickled specimens – fish, a sheep, a cow and calf, a shark entitled *The Physical Impossibility of Death in the Mind of Someone Living* (1991) – also dealt with the strength of human desire for and fear of love, beauty and death, and with our inadequacy in the face of them. Hirst bounces a ping-pong ball on a jet of air, like Koons's floating basketball, and calls it *I want to spend the rest of my life everywhere, with everyone, one to one, always, forever, now* (1991).

The American art world was preoccupied during the summer of

158

159

160 Andres Serrano
Piss Christ 1987

1989 with a debate over censorship. It concerned the work of two photographers, Robert Mapplethorpe (1946–89) and Andres Serrano (b. 1950). Over the preceding decade and a half, Mapplethorpe's figure studies, flowers, portraits and photo-constructions had explored male beauty, homosexual desire and sado-masochism. The tour of his retrospective, 'Robert Mapplethorpe: The Perfect Moment', came shortly after his death from AIDS-related illness and the publication of a book of his photographs that was denounced by, among others, Senator Jesse Helms. Serrano had made and was exhibiting a series of photographic studies involving various bodily fluids. One of these, a rich, golden-hued image of Christ on the cross, had been made by photographing a small plastic crucifix in a glass of urine. As the critic David Levi Strauss suggested it was probably less the image – which 'is really quite beautiful' – that upset people than the combination of words in its title, *Piss Christ* (1987). Both Mapplethorpe's retrospective and Serrano's series had been

161 Robert Mapplethorpe *Thomas, 1986* 1986

financed with assistance from public funds, a fact which was loudly deplored by morally outraged members of the Senate and the public. The debate encompassed issues of racism and sexism, as well as blasphemy and homophobia. The immediate result was that the House of Representatives reduced the National Endowment for the Arts's budget by the amount previously disbursed to the two projects, and Washington's Corcoran Gallery, scheduled as the third venue for Mapplethorpe's show, pulled out. Taking a leaf out of Krzysztof Wodiczko's book, Mapplethorpe's supporters staged a demonstration during which they projected slides of his work onto the gallery's façade, forcing it to 'house' the exhibition in spite of itself.

Over the same summer, that of 1989, the Centre Georges Pompidou in Paris held the exhibition *Magiciens de la Terre*. Containing work from all over the world, it aimed to show something of the heterogeneity of art, but also to answer charges of Eurocentrism by bringing together 'primitive' art and Western new art. New York's Museum of Modern Art had housed 'Primitivism in Twentieth-Century Art' back in 1984, an enterprise that aroused much criticism for its assumptions that art was a Western phenomenon feeding off the exotic and primitive it found elsewhere. The rationale for the MOMA exhibition maintained the notion of primitivism as the otherness to be found exclusively outside Western culture. It was as if the debates on racism, feminism and politics of the 1970s had never taken place, and as if the maturing of these discussions and their extension into other areas of social marginalization – notably those of sexual and gender identity brought to the fore in part by the onset of the AIDS crisis – were not, even then, having their effects. In spreading its curatorial net around the globe *Magiciens de la Terre* tried to present otherness as the stuff of a more equitable ideological exchange between cultures. Fifty Western and fifty non-Western artists were exhibited, the catalogue entry for each including a map showing their home as the centre of the world. The American critic Thomas McEvilley considered 'PC', the acronymic sign of late-1980s good behaviour, to stand for post-colonialism rather than political correctness. He wrote critically of 'Primitivism' in 1984, and much more supportively of *Magiciens*: 'All the criticism of the show that I have seen fails to confront the monumental fact that this was the first major exhibition consciously to attempt to

162 Cheri Samba *Les Capotes utilisées* 1990

discover a postcolonialist way to exhibit first- and third-world objects together. It was a major event in the social history of art, not in its aesthetic history.' How far the placing of objects together would lead to a *rapprochement* remained to be seen. The paintings of Zairean Cheri Samba (b. 1956) defined the size of the problem, their ironic texts remarking on Zaire's continuing economic dependency on France: 'Paris is clean thanks to us immigrants who don't like looking at piss and dog shit.' *Le Sida (AIDS)* (1989) suggested that while the threat from AIDS might be a global one we can neither afford to ignore the cultural traditions of the various places in which it occurs, nor pretend that the release of resources to combat it is triggered by humanitarian feeling and not political expediency.

In Britain, Rasheed Araeen (b. 1935) had long been similarly critical of the acquisitiveness and suppression of difference that underlay intercultural discourse. A work from the early 1980s, *I Love It, It Loves I* (1978–83), photographically documented the slaughter of a goat for the Muslim festival of Eid. Both subject matter and title pointed towards Beuys's *Coyote* and, by extension, the well-intentioned inclusiveness of Beuys's rhetoric expressed in his 'shamanistic' relationship to animals. They – a coyote here, a hare there – were able to comprehend the truths of art because of their proximity to the earth. Araeen's fields of old trainers, in the manner of Richard Long's lines of stones, driftwood, or other materials, questioned the validity of visiting 'other places' (other people's homes) merely in order to walk on them in the name of art.

As if in illustration of this tension, on the wall of the second site of *Magiciens* at La Villette, a large circular drawing executed in red mud

163 (left) Rasheed Araeen *A Long Walk in the Wilderness* 1991

164 (above) Richard Long *Red Earth Circle* 1989

by Richard Long is juxtaposed with a floor-painting in pigment on similar-coloured earth by the Yuendumu community of Alice Springs. Aboriginal paintings by artists including Michael Nelson Tjakamarra (b. 1949) and Clifford Possum Tjapaltjarri (b. 1932) from Papunya had become familiar during the 1980s because designs traditionally executed in sand were worked on canvas, often in acrylic paints, for exhibition and sale within the gallery system. In Australia, at least, this work was not an ethnographical curiosity but, as in the fish, rippling water and protruding sandbanks of Tjapaltjarri's *Fish Dreaming* (1986), or the peopled landscape of Tjakamarra's *Possum Dreaming* (1985), remained a distinct and distinctive means of conceptualizing and representing the world in visual terms. The landscapes of Tim Johnson (b. 1947) showed its influence, particularly in his *Antipodean Manifesto* (1986), and its imagery made frequent appearances, along with appropriations from Kiefer and

165 Adrian Piper *What It's Like, What It Is #3* 1991–92

166 David Hammons *Yo-yo* 1991

others, in the paintings of Imants Tillers. While he was happy that more people could now see his designs, Tjakamarra was convinced that their creation only remained possible because he and others who still lived outside the cities had not lost their culture: 'not like those people living in Sydney. They've lost all their culture, they just follow the European way,' he would say. Those in the cities, like Robert Campbell Jnr (b. 1944) and Gordon Bennett (b. 1955), may well have adopted more obviously European modes of image-making, but they used them in a trenchant critique of the colonialist appropriation of their continent.

Adrian Piper and David Hammons (b. 1943), who had been dealing with black nationalism since the early 1960s, continued at the same time to provide dextrous manipulation of Minimal and Conceptual strategies with a keen polemical edge. Both showed work in New York at the Museum of Modern Art's 1991 Installation exhibition '*Dislocations*'. The white, Minimal terracing around the walls in Piper's *What It's Like, What It Is #3* (1991–92) turned the room into an arena, in the centre of which was a tall column supporting a four-square arrangement of video monitors. On these a black man,

167 Sophie Calle *Last Seen: A Lady and Gentleman in Black by Rembrandt*
1991

periodically turning through ninety degrees, insistently informed the
spectator what he was not, stripping away one stereotype after another.
Hammons's *Public Enemy* (1991) showed photographs of an equestrian
statue of Theodore Roosevelt flanked by walking Native Americans.
These were defended by a ring of sandbagged gun emplacements, the
whole being heaped with piles of dead leaves and old party streamers
as a warning to those looking forward to celebrating the anniversary
of Columbus's landing the following year. Hammons was also a participant in the concurrently running Carnegie International in
Pittsburgh which that year was also devoted to Installation. The separ-
166   ate walls of *Yo-yo* (1991) had on them a delicately painted stencil
pattern redolent of yuppy domestic interior décor, and the random
marks made by a thrown ball. In the centre of the room a basketball,
gripped by the arms of a paint-mixing machine, vibrated to the music
of James Brown. Others who showed in Pittsburgh included Juan
Muñoz, Louise Bourgeois, whose cell-like rooms made of movable
screens carried forward her obsession with lairs, the French artist
Sophie Calle (b. 1953) and the Russian Ilya Kabakov (b. 1933). Calle
had previously gained notoriety for work which purported to involve
exploitation of an innocent public. The photo-text work *Suite*

204

Vénitienne (1983) narrates how she stalks a chance acquaintance whom she has overheard planning a trip to Venice. But this, like all her work, is a product of memory and imagination, concerned with desire and loss. *Last Seen: A Lady and Gentleman in Black by Rembrandt* (1991) was an attempt to retrieve through photographs and personal accounts the thirteen works of art, some by Vermeer and Rembrandt, which were stolen without trace from Boston's Isabella Stewart Gardner Museum in 1990. The critic David Deitcher's comment on the exhibition as a whole can be considered to be appropriate to Calle's work. 'Installation art,' he wrote, 'whether site-specific or not, has

168, 169
Exterior and interior
views of Ilya Kabakov's
The Toilet 1992

170 (left) Tony Oursler
Sexplotter (from *The Watching*)
1992 (detail)

171 (below) Gary Hill
Tall Ships 1992

172 (right) Stan Douglas
Hors-champs 1992

emerged as a flexible idiom; so flexible in fact that it can function all at once as a means of deconstructing the museum and of reconstructing it.' Unlike Vitali Komar (b. 1943) and Alexander Melamid (b. 1945), who left the Soviet Union for the US in the 1970s, following the bull-dozing of an unofficial, open-air exhibition of their work, Kabakov had stayed in Russia, working largely in secret until the collapse of communism. His installation at the Carnegie was the recreation of an old school complete with proudly displayed work by the pupils and

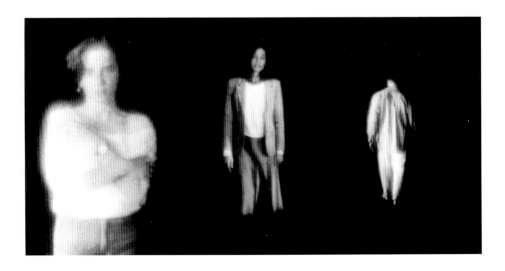

meticulously kept records of attendance and achievement. The school now, though, was empty following instructions that staff and pupils were to be moved to another, as yet unspecified, location. With this and other installations, such as the peasant home masquerading as a urinal he built behind Kassel's main museum for 1992's Documenta IX, Kabakov questions the wisdom of simply jettisoning seventy years of endeavour and expertise in obeisance to the West's superior economic wisdom.

168, 169

Some of the art which made the biggest impact at Documenta IX was the video work of Matthew Barney (b. 1967), Tony Oursler (b. 1957), Bill Viola (b. 1951), Gary Hill (b. 1951) and Stan Douglas (b. 1960). Visitors to a small storage space, deep in an underground car park, found *OTTOshaft* (1992): a large rubber mat, several prosthetic objects and other props together with two ceiling-mounted video monitors. The tape, which had been shot in the car park, featured Barney and others using the assembled props. Barney could also be seen on the tape climbing naked up the lift shaft with the aid of mountaineering tackle. Oursler's multi-part *The Watching*

(1992) spanned the Museum Fridericianum's stairwell from top to bottom. Shapeless bundles of material and clothes with stuffed cloth heads make up Oursler's dummies and effigies. The blank heads act as screens onto which videoed faces are projected, making them come to life as disturbing versions of the internal voices and media presences with whom we continually converse in our own heads. Viola showed *The Arc of Ascent* (1992), a huge, slow-motion projection of a man in loose clothing jumping into and floating around in a pool before, tape reversed, gathering all the air bubbles to himself and shooting off screen into darkness and silence. Our understanding of the body is a fundamental factor in Viola's art. It is 'the neglected key of our contemporary lives', and its trajectory from cradle to grave is pictured in his *Nantes Triptych* (1992) in which a similar floating figure is flanked on the left by film of Viola's wife giving birth to their son, and on the right by his mother, nearing death, lying on a hospital bed. Hill's *Tall Ships* (1992) was a broad, blacked-out corridor from the ceiling of which a line of video projectors cast silent black-and-white images obliquely down onto the walls. The films were of people approaching, looking with varying degrees of fascination at something – an object, scene or person, perhaps – and

171

173 Bill Viola *Nantes Triptych* 1992

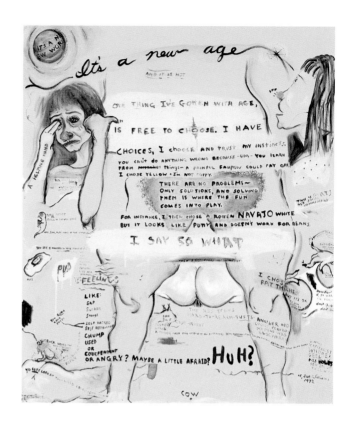

174 Sue Williams
The Yellow Painting 1992

retreating from it, the whole being at once the provocation for, an echo of, and a response to the viewer's behaviour. Hill described the work as bringing, in both a literal and figurative sense, 'slow illumination': 'As the figures come forth they provide the light in the space. Silhouettes of other viewers begin to appear. ...It's very subtle, but the viewers begin to mix with the projections.' For the filming of *Hors-champs* (1992), Douglas recreated a 1960s French TV studio setting for a free jazz improvisation featuring four black American musicians who had been based in Paris during that period. By editing between shots from two cameras, a 'broadcast' and an 'out-take' version of the session were obtained and projected onto either side of a screen suspended diagonally across the gallery. Neither version gave a full picture, and only one could be seen at a time.

172

The aesthetic and political resonance of the freedom exercised by black jazz musicians in their improvisations was also referred to by Lorna Simpson (b. 1960) in her installation for the 1993 Whitney

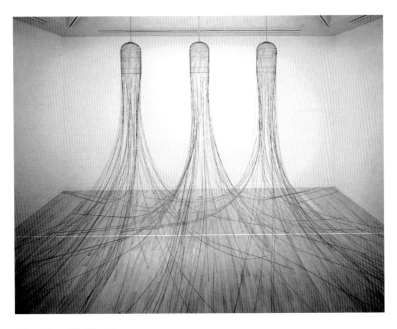

175 Pepe Espaliú *The Nest* 1993

Biennial. A wall of lips formed part of *Hypothetical*, a reflection on the implications and aftermath of the case in which police officers were prosecuted for beating up Rodney King. The *Village Voice* critic Greg Tate said of it: '*Hypothetical* invokes cuts like the [Miles] Davis Quintet's version of Herbie Hancock's "Riot" on 1967's *Nefertiti*. America's on fire and Miles and the crew are in some posh studio hideaway saying, Let's meditate on this in a succinct manner shall we?' Visitors to the 1993 Whitney Biennial were presented with a work by Daniel J. Martinez (b. 1957), a lapel badge bearing the slogan 'I CAN'T IMAGINE EVER WANTING TO BE WHITE'. It introduced an exhibition which consciously set out to emphasize, in the words of the curator Elizabeth Sussman, works that 'confront such dominant current issues as class, race, gender, sexuality and the family'. A quarter of a century after the agitational activities and protests of the Art Workers' Coalition, this would still lead the *New York Times* to conclude that such a show 'neglects painting', a verdict, as the critic Laura Cottingham suggested, that is equivalent to a charge of the absence of beauty and pleasure. The work of Sue Williams (b. 1954), one of the selected painters, suggested otherwise. Domestic and sexual drudgery, rape and physical violence against women are Williams's subject matter. Her images and words are treated in a raw illustrational and graphic style that owes a debt both to the crude directness of lavatory wall graffiti and the gestural discursiveness of Jackson Pollock. 'It's a new age and it's hot', paints Williams across *The Yellow Painting* (1992). 'One thing I've gotten with age, is free to choose.' And, over to one side, she has written: 'This is (art) not social commentary.' 174

Robert Gober's *Door with light bulb* installation (1992) containing his self-penned stories highlighting oppression and discrimination was also included at the 1993 Whitney Biennial and resurfaced as part of the 'Rites of Passage' exhibition at the Tate Gallery in 1995. The show's centrepiece was Beuys's *Terremoto in Palazzo*, the recreation of a 1981 installation that included a sawing horse precariously balanced on four glass jars. Broken glass covered the floor replicating the original occasion on which the jars Beuys was using to make the work fell and shattered. The exhibition's theme was the provisional and fragile nature of the body: photographic self- 177

176 Mona Hatoum *Light Sentence* 1992

177 Joseph Beuys *Terremoto in Palazzo* 1981

portraits of his ageing, naked body by John Coplans (b. 1920); Susan Hiller's *An Entertainment* (1990), which explored the brutally aggressive gender lessons taught by the children's Punch and Judy show; a Newton's cradle using glass ampoules filled with chlorine instead of the usual metal spheres by Hamad Butt (1962–94) and hugely extended, open-bottomed bird cages by Pepe Espaliú (1955–93), who, like Butt, had recently died from AIDS. *Corps Etranger* (1994) by Mona Hatoum (b. 1952) in which the video of an endoscopic journey through Hatoum's body is projected on the floor of a circular cubicle makes the viewer feel at once spectacularly intimate and at the same time distanced by the camera's dispassionate eye. A similarly disturbing effect had earlier been created by the changing size of the shadows in her *Light Sentence* (1992). The 'Passage' of the show's title is here between the solidity and certainty of the object and its dissolution into the flux of process. Art struggles to hold its place on the indeterminate ground that separates the two extremes.

Despite a burgeoning neo-conservative backlash in America and similar reactionary views in Britain and France, it's a new age. At the 1993 *Aperto*, the international exhibition for younger artists at the Venice Biennale, Rirkrit Tiravanija (b. 1961) installed tables and chairs and, with water boiled by two large gas burners, provided visitors with pots of instant noodles to eat. The title of the piece, *Untitled (Twelve Seventy One)*, referred to the year Marco Polo set off from Venice to visit China, the ultimate source of the food.

Tiravanija set up a bar the following year in the window of the SoHo gallery Metro Pictures. It dispensed free water rather than expensive coffee to those who wished to sit and watch the world go by. Noting a distinction between these gestures and the social utopianism of Matta-Clark's 'Food' restaurant, the critic Dan Cameron described them as: 'More ephemeral, less contained by the intricate relationships found in community infrastructures...Their particular nature as events arises from the placement of the spectator at the centre of the piece, allowing each one to determine the duration and nature of their interaction with the work at hand.' Viewers also find that they are unable to duck their responsibilities when confronting the work of Felix Gonzalez-Torres (b. 1957). Gonzalez-Torres, who died of AIDS in 1996, spread sweets in a square on the floor, or heaped them like a Minimalist corner piece in the angle of a room, and invited visitors to take one and eat it. His stacks of paper, equally Minimal in their formal derivation, induce more tension. '*Untitled*' *(Lover Boy)* (1990) is blue paper – blue for a boy, blue skies, heavenly blue – art still deals with beauty and longing and transcendence. You are allowed, if you wish, to take a sheet from the top of the pile, to consume not only the body of art, but also the body of the artist. The overtones are religious, sacramental, since the stack, constantly replenished, will not be exhausted. But what could you do with that piece of paper once you got it home to keep it as open and full of possibility as it was in the stack?

178 Felix Gonzalez-Torres '*Untitled*' *(Lover Boy)* 1990

Conclusion

The problem of what to do with the individual sheets of Gonzalez-Torres's stack of paper is ultimately one of responsibility. One is not confronted with the extreme and spectacular demands of the performances of Abramovic, Acconci, Pane, Burden and others, but the issue of the mutual obligations that exist between artist and spectator is equally present. To look at art is not to 'consume' it passively, but to become part of a world to which both that art and the spectator belong. Looking is not passive; it does not leave things unchanged.

The exhibitions mentioned in the last chapter were organized according to disparate agendas, curated with differing intent. Taken all in all, however, they demonstrate the extent to which the lines of aesthetic enquiry pursued during the preceding quarter of a century, far from trailing off or petering out, have become the essential vectors of today's art.

Two events in 1996 demonstrate this well. The first was *L'Informe: mode d'emploi*, a historical survey exhibition conceived by Rosalind Krauss and Yve-Alain Bois for the Centre Georges Pompidou in Paris. Taking as its starting point an idea from the writings of George Bataille, the exhibition offered a view of the changes in twentieth-century art that contrasted significantly with the traditional account of modernist development. The four main organizational categories within the show – Base Materialism, Pulse, Horizontality and Entropy – would be unthinkable without the practical and theoretical shifts of the past three decades. The second event, mounted at the Louisiana Arts Centre in Denmark and overseen by its director, Lars Nittve, was 'NowHere', which consisted of several independent shows, running concurrently, by an international group of young curators. In his catalogue introduction, *Nowhere but NowHere*, Nittve states: 'I was frightened, but also tempted. How to organize an exhibition that would acknowledge the changes of the last few decades, that would recognize an absence of structure, and that would work with small stories, with local language games and contexts? ...Might it be possible to make an exhibition a playground in which the differences – political, aesthetic, you name it – among the positions of contemporary artists and curators would be brought to the fore?'

The efforts of the 1960s and 1970s – in which artists sought to establish the political parameters of the artwork, to adapt the social marginality of modernist avant-garde practice into a means of voicing the experience of cultural marginality or of giving a voice to those who are, for various reasons, excluded from mainstream cultural experience – have by now been assimilated as significant factors in art's production and reception. There is a pulse in Warhol's imagery which is the pulse of the everyday, and there is a poetry in materials which Beuys and those who have come after him accept is inextricably bound up with the context of its utterance. How the artwork functions politically is not a question that can be answered independently of any consideration of its artistic merit. It is, rather, central to the way in which the work is able to exercise any aesthetic hold on the viewer at all. Art is a continuing reflective encounter with the world in which the work, far from being the end point of that process, acts as an initiator of and focus for the subsequent investigation of meaning.

Throughout the period covered here it has never been the case that perennial concerns for beauty, for the affecting qualities of form and for the search for a significance which appears to reach forward beyond the immediate present have been rejected. The struggle, rather, has been to find means to address those concerns that are appropriate to the character of contemporary life.

TIMELINE (durations indicated are approximate)

1960 **1970** **198**

Groups, Movements and Styles

- POP ART (STARTING IN MID-1950s) — NEO-EXPRESSIONISM
- ASSEMBLAGE (STARTING IN MID-1950s)
- NOUVEAU REALISME (NEW REALISM)
- ENVIRONMENTS AND HAPPENINGS
- POST-PAINTERLY ABSTRACTION
- OP, KINETIC AND LIGHT ART
- MINIMALISM
- CONCEPTUALISM
- PERFORMANCE
- PROCESS ART
- ARTE POVERA
- EARTH AND LAND ART
- PHOTOREALISM/HYPER REALISM

Influential Artists

Andre, Carl	**Manzoni**, Piero	**Acconci**, Vito	**Kounellis**, Jannis
Artschwager, Richard	**Noland**, Kenneth	**Art & Language**	**LeWitt**, Sol
Caro, Anthony	**Oldenburg**, Claes	**Baselitz**, Georg	**Long**, Richard
Flavin, Dan	**Rauschenberg**, Robert	**Beuys**, Joseph	**Merz**, Mario
Fluxus Group	**Reinhardt**, Ad	**Buren**, Daniel	**Nauman,** Bruce
Johns, Jasper	**Riley**, Bridget	**Christo** & Jeanne-Claude	**Penone**, Giuseppe
Judd, Donald	**Rosenquist**, James	**Gilbert and George**	**Polke**, Sigmar
Kelly, Ellsworth	**Ruscha**, Edward	**Haacke**, Hans	**Richter**, Gerhard
Kienholz, Ed	**Stella**, Frank	**Hesse**, Eva	**Ryman**, Robert
Klein, Yves	**Tinguely**, Jean	**Immendorff**, Jörg	**Serra**, Richard
Lichtenstein, Roy	**Warhol**, Andy	**Kelly**, Mary	**Smithson**, Robert
Louis, Morris	**Wesselman**, Tom	**Kosuth**, Joseph	**Weiner**, Lawrence

Important Events

1960 • Claes Oldenburg, *The Street*
 • Andy Warhol, *Dick Tracy*, first comic strip painting
 • Yves Klein, *anthropométries*
 • Pierre Restany, New Realist Manifesto
1961 • *The Art of Assemblage* exhib., MOMA, NY
 • Clement Greenberg publishes *Art and Culture*
 • Claes Oldenburg, *The Store*
 • Fluxus group formed
 • John F. Kennedy elected President of US
 • Berlin Wall constructed
 • Yuri Gagarin first man in space
1962 • Warhol paints Marilyn Monroe and Campbell's Soup cans; first major exhib., LA
 • Edward Ruscha, *Twenty-Six Gasoline Stations*
 • Death of Yves Klein
1963 • Assassination of President Kennedy
 • Duchamp retrospective, Pasadena
 • *Towards a New Abstraction* exhib., LA
 • Death of Piero Manzoni
1964 • *Post-painterly Abstraction* exhib., LA
 • Venice Biennale – Rauschenberg awarded first prize
 • Carolee Schneeman, *Meat Joy*, NY
1965 • Warhol retrospective, Pennsylvania, US
 • Beuys, *Twenty-Four Hours*, Wuppertal, Germany
 • National Endowment for the Arts (NEA) founded, US
1966 • *Primary Structures* exhib., Jewish Museum, NY
1967 • Marshall McLuhan, *The Medium is the Message*
 • Che Guevara killed in Bolivia
1968 • Death of Marcel Duchamp
 • Assassination of Martin Luther King
 • *Les événements* – student rioting in Paris
1969 • *Arte Povera*, term coined by Germano Celant
 • *Anti-Illusion: Procedures/Materials* exhib., Whitney Museum, NY
 • *When Attitudes Become Form* exhib., Berne, Krefeld, and London
 • *Nine at Castelli* exhib. org. by Robert Morris, NY
 • First issue of *Art-Language*
 • Stonewall gay riot, NY

1970 • *Information* exhib., MOMA, NY
 • Robert Smithson, *Spiral Jetty*, Great Salt Lake, Utah
1971 • *Contemporary Black Artists in America* exhib., Whitney Museum, NY
1972 • Documenta V: *Individual Myths – Parallel Picture Worlds*, Kassel
1973 • Salvador Allende overthrown in Chile
1976 • *Women Artists: 1550–1950* exhib., Los Angeles County Museum of Art
1977 • Walter de Maria, *Lightning Field*, New Mexico
 • Documenta VI: *Art and Media*, Kassel
 • Opening of the Centre Georges Pompidou, Paris
 • First *Skulptur Projekt* exhib., Münster
1978 • *Bad Painting* exhib., New Museum of Contemporary Art, NY
1979 • Joseph Beuys retrospective exhib., Guggenheim Museum, NY
 • Judy Chicago, *The Dinner Party*

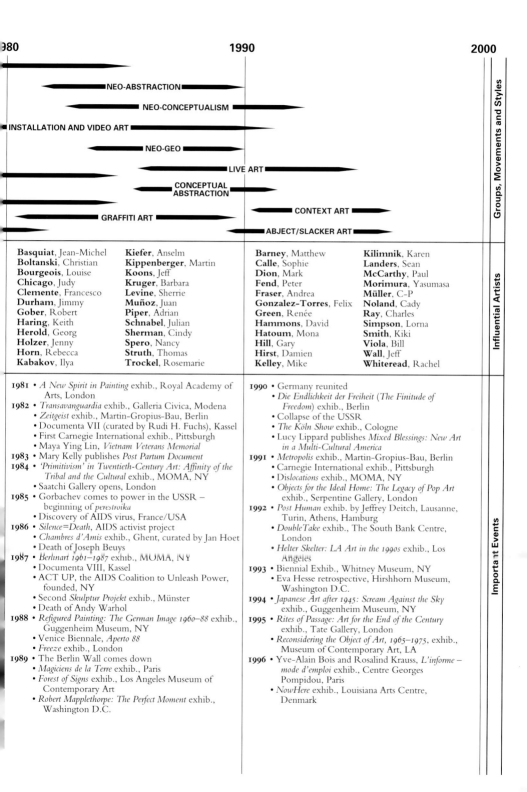

Groups, Movements and Styles

- NEO-ABSTRACTION
- NEO-CONCEPTUALISM
- INSTALLATION AND VIDEO ART
- NEO-GEO
- LIVE ART
- CONCEPTUAL ABSTRACTION
- GRAFFITI ART
- CONTEXT ART
- ABJECT/SLACKER ART

Influential Artists

Basquiat, Jean-Michel	**Kiefer**, Anselm	**Barney**, Matthew	**Kilimnik**, Karen
Boltanski, Christian	**Kippenberger**, Martin	**Calle**, Sophie	**Landers**, Sean
Bourgeois, Louise	**Koons**, Jeff	**Dion**, Mark	**McCarthy**, Paul
Chicago, Judy	**Kruger**, Barbara	**Fend**, Peter	**Morimura**, Yasumasa
Clemente, Francesco	**Levine**, Sherrie	**Fraser**, Andrea	**Müller**, C-P
Durham, Jimmy	**Muñoz**, Juan	**Gonzalez-Torres**, Felix	**Noland**, Cady
Gober, Robert	**Piper**, Adrian	**Green**, Renée	**Ray**, Charles
Haring, Keith	**Schnabel**, Julian	**Hammons**, David	**Simpson**, Lorna
Herold, Georg	**Sherman**, Cindy	**Hatoum**, Mona	**Smith**, Kiki
Holzer, Jenny	**Spero**, Nancy	**Hill**, Gary	**Viola**, Bill
Horn, Rebecca	**Struth**, Thomas	**Hirst**, Damien	**Wall**, Jeff
Kabakov, Ilya	**Trockel**, Rosemarie	**Kelley**, Mike	**Whiteread**, Rachel

Important Events

1981 • *A New Spirit in Painting* exhib., Royal Academy of Arts, London

1982 • *Transavanguardia* exhib., Galleria Civica, Modena
• *Zeitgeist* exhib., Martin-Gropius-Bau, Berlin
• Documenta VII (curated by Rudi H. Fuchs), Kassel
• First Carnegie International exhib., Pittsburgh
• Maya Ying Lin, *Vietnam Veterans Memorial*

1983 • Mary Kelly publishes *Post Partum Document*

1984 • *'Primitivism' in Twentieth-Century Art: Affinity of the Tribal and the Cultural* exhib., MOMA, NY
• Saatchi Gallery opens, London

1985 • Gorbachev comes to power in the USSR – beginning of *perestroika*
• Discovery of AIDS virus, France/USA

1986 • *Silence=Death*, AIDS activist project
• *Chambres d'Amis* exhib., Ghent, curated by Jan Hoet
• Death of Joseph Beuys

1987 • *Berlinart 1961–1987* exhib., MOMA, NY
• Documenta VIII, Kassel
• ACT UP, the AIDS Coalition to Unleash Power, founded, NY
• Second *Skulptur Projekt* exhib., Münster
• Death of Andy Warhol

1988 • *Refigured Painting: The German Image 1960–88* exhib., Guggenheim Museum, NY
• Venice Biennale, *Aperto 88*
• *Freeze* exhib., London

1989 • The Berlin Wall comes down
• *Magiciens de la Terre* exhib., Paris
• *Forest of Signs* exhib., Los Angeles Museum of Contemporary Art
• *Robert Mapplethorpe: The Perfect Moment* exhib., Washington D.C.

1990 • Germany reunited
• *Die Endlichkeit der Freiheit* (*The Finitude of Freedom*) exhib., Berlin
• Collapse of the USSR
• *The Köln Show* exhib., Cologne
• Lucy Lippard publishes *Mixed Blessings: New Art in a Multi-Cultural America*

1991 • *Metropolis* exhib., Martin-Gropius-Bau, Berlin
• Carnegie International exhib., Pittsburgh
• *Dislocations* exhib., MOMA, NY
• *Objects for the Ideal Home: The Legacy of Pop Art* exhib., Serpentine Gallery, London

1992 • *Post Human* exhib. by Jeffrey Deitch, Lausanne, Turin, Athens, Hamburg
• *DoubleTake* exhib., The South Bank Centre, London
• *Helter Skelter: LA Art in the 1990s* exhib., Los Angeles

1993 • Biennial Exhib., Whitney Museum, NY
• Eva Hesse retrospective, Hirshhorn Museum, Washington D.C.

1994 • *Japanese Art after 1945: Scream Against the Sky* exhib., Guggenheim Museum, NY

1995 • *Rites of Passage: Art for the End of the Century* exhib., Tate Gallery, London
• *Reconsidering the Object of Art, 1965–1975*, exhib., Museum of Contemporary Art, LA

1996 • Yve-Alain Bois and Rosalind Krauss, *L'informe – mode d'emploi* exhib., Centre Georges Pompidou, Paris
• *NowHere* exhib., Louisiana Arts Centre, Denmark

Select Bibliography

Chapter One

Baker, K., *Minimalism: Art of Circumstance*, N.Y., 1988

Battcock, G., *The New Art: A Critical Anthology*, N.Y., 1966; ed., *Minimal Art: A Critical Anthology*, N.Y., 1968

Crane, D., *The Transformation of the Avant-Garde: The New York Art World: 1940–1985*, Chicago, 1987

Foster, H., *The Return of the Real: The Avant-Garde at the End of the Century*, Cambridge, Mass., 1996

Frascina, F., ed., *Pollock and After: The Critical Debate*, N.Y., 1985

Fried, M., *Three American Painters*, Cambridge, Mass., 1965

Geldzahler, H., *New York Painting and Sculpture: 1940–1970*, N.Y., 1969

Hertz, R., ed., *Theories of Contemporary Art*, Englewood Cliffs, N.J., 1985

Judd, D., *Complete Writings 1959–75*, Halifax, Nova Scotia & N.Y., 1975

Kuspit, D., *The Cult of the Avant-Garde Artist*, N.Y., 1996

Lippard, L. R., *Pop Art*, N.Y. & London, 1966

McShine, K., ed., *Andy Warhol: A Retrospective*, N.Y. & Boston, 1989

Restany, P., 'Le Nouveau Réalisme à la Conquête de New York', in *Art International*, January 1963

Russell, J., & S. Gablik, *Pop Art Redefined*, London, 1969

Sandler, I., *Art of the Postmodern Era: From the Late 60s to the Early 90s*, N.Y., 1996

Spoerri, D., *An Anecdoted Topography of Chance*, N.Y., 1966; London, 1995

Swenson, G., *What is Pop Art?*, in *Art News*, November 1963 & February 1964

Waldman, D., *Collage, Assemblage and the Found Object*, N.Y., 1992

Warhol, A., *The Philosophy of Andy Warhol: From A to B and Back Again*, N.Y., 1975

Chapter Two

Aliaga, J. V., & J. M. Cortes, eds, *Arte Conceptual Revisado (Conceptual Art Revisited)*, Valencia, 1990

Archer, M. (intro.), N. de Oliveira, N. Oxley & M. Petry, *Installation Art*, London & Washington D.C., 1994

Battcock, G., ed., *Idea Art: A Critical Anthology*, N.Y., 1973; with R. Nickas, eds, *The Art of Performance: A Critical Anthology*, N.Y., 1984

Beardsley, J., *Earthworks and Beyond*, N.Y., 1989

Celant, G., *Arte Povera: Conceptual, Actual or Impossible Art?*, Milan & London, 1969; *The Knot: Arte Povera at P.S.1*, N.Y., 1985

Concept Art, Minimal, Arte Povera, Land Art, Stuttgart, 1990

Cooke, L., & M. Francis, *Carnegie International 1991*, N.Y., 1992

Goldberg, R., *Performance Art*, London & N.Y., 1988

Goldstein, A., & A. Rorimer, eds, *Reconsidering the Object of Art: 1965–1975*, L.A. Museum of Contemporary Art, Boston, 1995

Graham, D., *Rock My Religion: Writings and Projects 1965–90*, Boston, 1993

Harrison, C., *Essays on Art & Language*, Oxford, 1991

Hoet, Jan, *Chambres d'Amis*, Ghent, 1986

Holt, N., ed., *The Writings of Robert Smithson*, N.Y., 1979

Kosuth, J., *Art After Philosophy and After: Collected Writings 1966–1990*, Cambridge, Mass., 1991

Krauss, R., *Passages in Modern Sculpture*, London & N.Y., 1977

Lippard, L. R., *Overlay: Contemporary Art and the Art of Prehistory*, N.Y., 1983; *Six Years: The Dematerialisation of the Art Object from 1966 to 1972*, London, 1973

McShine, K., ed., *Information*, N.Y., 1970

Meyer, U., *Conceptual Art*, N.Y., 1972

Morgan, R. C., *Art Into Ideas: Essays on Conceptual Art*, Cambridge, N.Y., & Melbourne, 1996

O'Doherty, B., *Inside the White Cube: The Ideology of the Gallery Space*, San Francisco, 1986

Pincus-Witten, R., *Postminimalism into Maximalism: American Art, 1966–1986*, Ann Arbor, 1987

Sayre, H., *The Object of Performance: The American Avant-Garde Since 1970*, Chicago, 1989

Sonfist, A., ed., *Art on the Land: A Critical Anthology of Environmental Art*, N.Y., 1983

Szeeman, H., *Live in Your Head – When Attitudes Become Form: Works, Concepts, Processes, Situations, Information*, Bern, 1969

Chapter Three

Baker, E., & T. Hess, eds, *Art and Sexual Politics: Women's Liberation, Women Artists and Art History*, N.Y., 1973

Battcock, G., ed., *Super-Realism*, N.Y., 1975; ed., *New Artists Video: A Critical Anthology*, N.Y., 1978; with R. Nickas, eds, *The Art of Performance: A Critical Anthology*, N.Y., 1984

Broude, N., & M. D. Garrard, eds, *The Power of Feminist Art*, N.Y. & London, 1994

Chadwick, W., *Women, Art, and Society*, London & N.Y., rev. ed., 1996

Chicago, J., *The Dinner Party: A Symbol of Our Heritage*, Garden City, N.Y., 1979; *Through the Flower: My Struggle as a Woman Artist*, N.Y., 1975

Cockroft, E., J. Weber & J. Cockroft, *Toward a People's Art: The Contemporary Mural Movement*, N.Y., 1977

Hendricks, J., ed., *Fluxus Codex*, Detroit & N.Y., 1988

Kellein, T., & J. Hendricks, *Fluxus*, London, 1995

Levin, K., *Beyond Modernism: Essays on Art from the '70s and '80s*, N.Y., 1988

Lippard, L. R., *From the Center: Feminist Essays on Women's Art*, N.Y., 1976; *Get the Message? A Decade of Art for Social Change*, N.Y., 1984

Nochlin, L., 'Why Have There Been No Great Women Artists?' in *Women, Art, and Power and Other Essays*, London & N.Y., 1989

Oliva, A. B., ed., *Ubi Fluxus Ibi Motus 1990-1962*, 44th Venice Biennale, Milan, 1990

Parker, R., & G. Pollock, *Old Mistresses: Women, Art and Ideology*, London, 1981

Pollock, G., *Vision and Difference: Femininity, Feminism and the Histories of Art*, London, 1988

Popper, F., *Art, Action and Participation*, N.Y., 1975

Tisdall, C., *Joseph Beuys*, N.Y., 1979

Wallis, B., ed., *If You Lived Here: The City in Art, Theory, and Social Activism*, Discussions in Contemporary Culture 6, Seattle, 1991

Weyergraf-Serra, C., & M. Suskirk, eds, *The Destruction of Tilted Arc*, Boston, 1991

Chapters Four & Five

Bois, Y.-A., *Painting as Model*, Boston, 1990; with R. Krauss, *L'Informe: mode d'emploi*, Centre Georges Pompidou, Paris, 1996

Buchloh, B., ed., *Broodthaers: Writings, Interviews, Photographs*, Boston, 1988

Cameron, D., *NY Art Now: The Saatchi Collection*, London, 1988

Crimp, D., & A. Rolston, *AIDS Demo Graphics*, Seattle, 1990

Deitch, J., et al., *The Dakis Joannou Collection*, N.Y. & Ostfildern, 1996

Foster, H., ed., *The Anti-Aesthetic: Essays in Postmodern Culture*, Seattle, 1983; *Recodings: Art, Spectacle, Cultural Politics*, Seattle, 1985; ed., Discussions in Contemporary Culture 1, Seattle, 1987; ed., *Vision and Visuality*, Discussions in Contemporary Culture 2, Seattle, 1988

Gudis, C., ed., *A Forest of Signs: Art in the Crisis of Representation*, Boston, 1989

Joachimedes, C., ed., *A New Spirit in Painting*, London, 1981

Joselit, D., & E. Sussman, eds, *Endgame: Reference and Simulation in Recent Painting and Sculpture*, Boston, 1986

Kuspit, D., *Signs of Psyche in Modern and Postmodern Art*, N.Y., 1996

Livingstone, M., *Pop Art: A Continuing History*, London, 1990

McEvilley, T., *Art and Otherness: Crisis in Cultural Identity*, N.Y., 1992; *The Exile's Return: Toward a Redefinition of Painting for the Postmodern Era*, Cambridge, 1993

Magiciens de la Terre, Centre Georges Pompidou, Paris, 1989

Michelson, A., et al., eds, *'October': The First Decade*, Boston, 1987

Modern Dreams: The Rise and Fall and Rise of Pop, Cambridge, Mass., 1988

Oliva, A. B., *La Transavanguardia Internazionale*, Milan, 1982

Owens, C., *Beyond Recognition: Representation, Power, and Culture*, Berkeley, 1992

Popper, F., *Art of the Electronic Age*, London & N.Y., 1993

Powell, R. E., *Black Art and Culture in the Twentieth Century*, London & N.Y., 1997

Refigured Painting: The German Image 1960–88, Solomon R. Guggenheim Museum, N.Y., 1988

Saltz, J., ed., *Beyond Boundaries: New York's New Art*, N.Y., 1986

Stiles, K., & P. Selz, *Theories and Documents of Contemporary Art: A Sourcebook of Artists' Writings*, Berkeley, L.A. & London, 1996

Tomkins, C., *Post to Neo: The Art World of the 80s*, N.Y., 1988

Wallis, B., ed., *Art After Modernism: Rethinking Representation*, N.Y. & Boston, 1984; with T. Finkelpearl, eds, *This is Tomorrow Today: The Independent Group and British Pop Art*, N.Y., 1987

Zeitgeist, Martin-Gropius-Bau, Berlin, 1982

List of Illustrations

Measurements are given in centimetres, followed by inches, height before width before depth, unless otherwise stated

1 Robert Rauschenberg *Bed* 1955. Combine painting: oil and pencil on pillow, quilt, and sheet on wood supports 191.1 x 80 x 20.3 ($75\frac{1}{4}$ x $31\frac{1}{2}$ x 8). The Museum of Modern Art, New York. Gift of Leo Castelli in honor of Alfred H. Barr, Jr. Photo © 1997 The Museum of Modern Art, New York. © Robert Rauschenberg/DACS, London/VAGA, New York 1997
2 Jean Tinguely *Homage to New York* 1960. Mixed media, destroyed. Photo © David Gahr 1960. © ADAGP, Paris and DACS, London 1997
3 Robert Rauschenberg *Buffalo II* 1964. Oil and silkscreen ink on canvas 243.9 x 182.9 (96 x 72). Private collection. © Robert Rauschenberg/DACS, London/VAGA, New York 1997
4 Jasper Johns *Flag* 1954–55; dated on reverse 1954. Encaustic, oil and collage on fabric mounted on plywood 107.3 x 153.8 ($42\frac{1}{4}$ x $60\frac{5}{8}$). The Museum of Modern Art, New York. Gift of Philip Johnson in honor of Alfred H. Barr, Jr. Photo © 1997 The Museum of Modern Art, New York. © Jasper Johns/DACS, London/VAGA, New York 1997
5 Roy Lichtenstein *I Know How You Must Feel, Brad* 1963. Oil and magna on canvas 168.9 x 95.9 ($66\frac{1}{2}$ x $37\frac{3}{4}$). The Ludwig Collection, Wallraf-Richartz Museum, Cologne. © Roy Lichtenstein/DACS 1997
6 James Rosenquist *F-111* 1965. Oil, canvas and aluminium 3.05 x 26.21 m. (10 x 86 ft.). Private collection. Photo Rudolf Burckhardt. © James Rosenquist/DACS, London/VAGA, New York 1997
7 Andy Warhol *Do-It-Yourself (Flowers)* 1962. Synthetic polymer paint, type and pencil on canvas 175 x 150 (69 x 59). Private collection. Photo courtesy Alesco AG, Zurich. © ARS, NY and DACS, London 1997
8 Andy Warhol *Brillo Boxes* 1964. Silkscreen ink on wood, each box 43.5 x 43.5 x 35.6 ($17\frac{1}{8}$ x $17\frac{1}{8}$ x 14). Installed at the Stable Gallery, 1964. Photo John Schiff. Courtesy The Andy Warhol Foundation for the Visual Arts, Inc. © ARS, NY and DACS, London 1997
9 Roy Lichtenstein *Little Big Painting* 1965. Oil and magna on canvas 172.7 x 203.2 (68 x 80). Whitney Museum of American Art, New York. Photo Rudolf Burckhardt. © Roy Lichtenstein/DACS 1997
10 Claes Oldenburg *The Store*, 107 East Second Street, New York, December 1961 (interior view). Courtesy the artist
11 Tom Wesselmann *Great American Nude No. 54* 1964. Museum Moderner Kunst Stiftung Ludwig, Vienna, formerly Hahn Collection, Cologne. © Tom Wesselmann/DACS, London/VAGA, New York 1997
12 Ed Kienholz *Roxy's* 1961. Mixed media assemblage, various dimensions. Courtesy L. A. Louver Gallery, Venice, California
13 Edward Ruscha *Los Angeles County Museum On Fire* 1965–68. Oil on canvas 137.2 x 335.28 (54 x 132). Collection Hirshhorn Museum & Sculpture Garden, Washington, D.C. Courtesy the artist
14 David Hockney *The Most Beautiful Boy in the World* 1961. Oil on canvas 177.8 x 100.3 (70 x $39\frac{1}{2}$). Collection Werner Boeninger. © David Hockney
15 Jesús Rafaël Soto *Cube of Ambiguous Space* 1969. Plexiglass and paint 250 x 250 x 250 ($88\frac{1}{2}$ x $88\frac{1}{2}$ x $88\frac{1}{2}$). Soto Foundation, Soto Museum, Ciudad Bolívar, Venezuela. Courtesy the artist
16 Victor Vasarely, plate 2 from the portfolio *Planetary Folklore* 1964. Serigraph, printed in colour, composition: 62.7 x 60 ($24\frac{11}{16}$ x $23\frac{5}{8}$). The Museum of Modern Art, New York. Larry Aldrich Fund. Photo © 1997 The Museum of Modern Art, New York. © ADAGP, Paris and DACS, London 1997
17 Bridget Riley *Twist* 1963. Emulsion on wood 121.9 x 116.2 (48 x $45\frac{3}{4}$). Courtesy the artist
18 Günther Uecker *Kreis, Kreise* 1970. Painted nails on wood 149.9 x 149.9 (59 x 59). Stiftung Ludwig Roselius Museum, on loan to the Neues Museum Weserburg, Bremen. Photo © Jörg Michaelis, Bremen
19 Michelangelo Pistoletto *Two People* 1962. Painted tissue paper on mirrored stainless steel 200 x 120 ($78\frac{3}{4}$ x $47\frac{1}{4}$). Private collection, New York. Photo P. Bressano, Turin. Courtesy Maria and Michelangelo Pistoletto
20 César (César Baldaccini) *The Yellow Buick* 1961. Compressed automobile 151.1 x 77.7 x 63.5 ($59\frac{1}{2}$ x $30\frac{3}{4}$ x $24\frac{7}{8}$). The Museum of Modern Art, New York. Gift of Mr. and Mrs. John Rewald. Photo © 1997 The Museum of Modern Art, New York. © ADAGP, Paris and DACS, London 1997
21 John Chamberlain *Miss Lucy Pink* 1963. Painted steel 119.4 x 106.7 x 99.1 (47 x 42 x 39). Photo courtesy PaceWildenstein, New York. © ARS, NY and DACS, London 1997
22 Arman (Armand P. Arman) *Arteriosclerose* 1961. Accumulation of forks and spoons in a box 47.5 x 72.5 x 7.5 ($18\frac{3}{4}$ x $28\frac{5}{8}$ x 3). © ADAGP, Paris and DACS, London 1997
23 Yayoi Kusama *Air Mail Stickers* 1962. Collage on canvas 181.6 x 171.5 ($71\frac{1}{2}$ x $67\frac{1}{2}$). Whitney Museum of American Art, New York. Gift of Mr. Hanford Yang, Acc. No. 64.34. Photo © 1996 Whitney Museum of American Art, New York. Photo Pierre Dupuy, Stamford, Connecticut
24 Yves Klein *Celebration of a New Anthropometric Era* 1960. Paint on canvas, life-size bodyprints. Courtesy Galerie Karl Flinker, Paris. Photo Jean Dubout, Paris. © ADAGP, Paris and DACS, London 1997
25 Piero Manzoni making *The Artist's Breath* 1961
26 Konrad Lueg and Gerhard Richter *A Demonstration for Capitalist Realism*, Bergeshaus, Flingerstraße 11, Düsseldorf, 11 October 1963. Photo courtesy Konrad Fischer, Düsseldorf
27 Gerhard Richter *Olympia* 1967. Oil on canvas 200 x 130 ($78\frac{3}{4}$ x $51\frac{1}{4}$). Private collection
28 Sigmar Polke *Moderne Kunst* 1968. Acrylic and oil on canvas 150 x 125 (59 x $49\frac{1}{4}$). Courtesy René Block, Berlin
29 Wolf Vostell *Berlin–Fieber V* 1973. 130 x 120 ($51\frac{1}{8}$ x $47\frac{1}{4}$). Photo courtesy Galerie Inge Baecker, Cologne. © DACS 1997
30 Andy Warhol *Silver Disaster: Electric Chair* 1963. Acrylic and silkscreen on canvas 100 x 150 (42 x 60). Sonnabend Collection, New York. © ARS, NY and DACS, London 1997
31 Morris Louis *Omicron* 1961. Synthetic polymer paint on canvas 262.3 x 412 ($103\frac{1}{4}$ x $162\frac{1}{4}$). Photo Waddington Gallery, London
32 Kenneth Noland *Song* 1958. Synthetic polymer 165.1 x 165.1 (65 x 65). Whitney Museum of American Art, New York. © Kenneth Noland/DACS, London/VAGA, New York 1997
33 Ellsworth Kelly *Orange and Green* 1966. Oil on canvas 223.5 x 165.1 (88 x 65). Courtesy Sidney Janis Gallery, New York
34 Richard Smith *Tailspan* 1965. Acrylic on wood 119.9 x 212.7 x 90.2 ($47\frac{1}{4}$ x $83\frac{3}{4}$ x $35\frac{1}{2}$). © Tate Gallery, London
35 Anthony Caro *Prairie* 1967. Steel painted yellow 96.5 x 581.7 x 320 (38 x 229 x 126). Private collection. Courtesy the artist
36 Phillip King *Genghis Khan* 1963. Purple reinforced plastic 213.4 x 365.8 (84 x 144). Private collection. Courtesy the artist
37 Robert Morris *Untitled (Slab)* 1968 (reconstruction of first version in plywood 1962). Painted steel 243.8 x 243.8 x 20.3 (96 x 96 x 8). © ARS, NY and DACS, London 1997
38 Donald Judd *Untitled* 1965. Galvanized iron and aluminium 83.8 x 358.1 x 76.2 (33 x 141 x 30). Private collection. Photo Rudolf Burckhardt. © ARS, NY and DACS, London 1997
39 Barnett Newman *Who's Afraid of Red, Yellow and Blue III* 1966–67. Oil on canvas 243.8 x 543.56 (96 x 214). Stedelijk Museum, Amsterdam. Photo courtesy The Barnett Newman Foundation, New York
40 Frank Stella *Getty's Tomb, II* 1959. Enamel on canvas 213.4 x 243.8 (84 x 96). Los Angeles County Museum of Art, Los Angeles, California (purchased with Contemporary Art Council funds). © ARS, NY and DACS, London 1997
41 Donald Judd's permanent installation of works, East Building, La Mansana de Chinati, Marfa, Texas. Photo courtesy Donald Judd Estate. © ARS, NY and DACS, London 1997
42 Donald Judd *Untitled* 1968. Amber, plexiglass and stainless steel 83.8 x 172.7 x 121.9 (33 x 68 x 48). Photo courtesy Donald Judd Estate. © ARS, NY and DACS, London 1997
43 Frank Stella *Delaware Crossing* from 'Benjamin Moore' series 1961. Alkyd on canvas 195.6 x 195.6 (77 x 77). Private collection. © ARS, NY and DACS, London 1997
44 Dan Flavin *The Nominal Three (To William of Ockham)* 1963. Fluorescent light, overall size 182.8 x 133.3 (72 x $52\frac{1}{2}$). Solomon R. Guggenheim Museum, New York. Photo David Heald © The Solomon R. Guggenheim Foundation, New York. FN 91.3698. © ARS, NY and DACS, London 1997
45 Carl Andre *Equivalents I–VIII* 1966. Sand-lime bricks each 6.4 x 11.4 x 22.9 ($2\frac{1}{2}$ x $4\frac{1}{2}$ x 9). Installed at Tibor de Nagy Gallery, New York, 1966. Photo courtesy Paula Cooper

Gallery, New York. © Carl Andre/DACS, London/VAGA, New York 1997
46 Carl Andre *37 Pieces of Work* Fall 1969. Aluminium, copper, steel, lead, magnesium and zinc; total size 10.97 x 10.97 m. (36 x 36 ft.): 1296 units, 216 of each metal, each unit 30.5 x 30.5 x 1.9 (12 x 12 x ¾). Collection Dwan Gallery, New York. As installed for the exhibition *Carl Andre* on the rotunda floor of the Solomon R. Guggenheim Museum, New York. Photo Robert E. Mates and Paul Katz. Photo © The Solomon R. Guggenheim Foundation, New York. © Carl Andre/DACS, London/VAGA, New York 1997
47 Robert Morris *Untitled* 1965. Plexiglass mirror on wood, four pieces each 71.1 x 71.1 x 71.1 (28 x 28 x 28). Installed at Green Gallery, New York, February 1965. © ARS, NY and DACS, London 1997
48 Richard Serra *One Ton Prop (House of Cards)* 1968–69. Lead plates each 139.7 x 139.7 (55 x 55). Private collection. © ARS, NY and DACS, London 1997
49 Eva Hesse *Hang Up* 1966. Acrylic on cloth, wood and steel 182.8 x 213.3 x 198.1 (72 x 84 x 78). The Art Institute of Chicago. © Estate of Eva Hesse. Courtesy Robert Miller Gallery, New York
50 Eva Hesse *Accretion* 1968. Fibreglass and polyester resin, 50 units each 148.6 x 6.3 (58½ x 2½). Kröller-Müller Museum, Otterlo, The Netherlands. © Estate of Eva Hesse. Courtesy Robert Miller Gallery, New York
51 John McCracken *There's No Reason Not To* 1967. Wood and fibreglass 304.8 x 45.7 x 8.9 (120 x 18 x 3½). Nicholas Wilder Gallery, Los Angeles
52 Lynda Benglis *For Carl Andre* 1970. Pigmented polyurethane foam 142.9 x 135.3 x 118.11 (56¼ x 53¼ x 46½). Collection of the Modern Art Museum of Fort Worth, Fort Worth, Texas. Museum purchase, The Benjamin J. Tillar Memorial Trust. © Lynda Benglis/DACS, London/VAGA, New York 1997
53 Bruce Nauman *Composite Photo of Two Messes on the Studio Floor* 1967. Gelatin-silver print 102.9 x 312.4 (40½ x 123). The Museum of Modern Art, New York. Gift of Philip Johnson. Photo © 1997 The Museum of Modern Art, New York. © ARS, NY and DACS, London 1997
54 Barry Flanagan *four casb 2'67, ring/1'67, rope (gr 2sp 60) 6'67* 1967. Cloth, 32 x 52 x 48 (12½ x 20½ x 19). Arts Council Collection, London
55 Niele Toroni *Présentation: imprints of a no. 50 brush repeated at regular intervals of 30 cm* 1966–96. Courtesy the artist
56 Sol LeWitt *Four basic kinds of straight lines and their combinations* 1969. Courtesy Lisson Gallery, London. © ARS, NY and DACS, London 1997
57 Sol LeWitt *Four basic colours and their combinations* 1971. Courtesy Lisson Gallery, London. © ARS, NY and DACS, London 1997
58 Daniel Buren *Opéra* from *Legend I* April 1970. Photograph album, Warehouse Publications, London 1973. © Daniel Buren, 1973. © ADAGP, Paris and DACS, London 1997
59 On Kawara *I am still alive* and a response from Sol LeWitt. Projects for Lucy R. Lippard's contribution to *July/August Exhibition Book*, organized by Seth Siegelaub and presented in *Studio International* (July–August 1970), pp. 36–37
60 Lawrence Weiner *A 36" x 36" removal to the lathing or support wall of plaster or wallboard from a wall* 1968. Collection of the Siegelaub Collection & Archives. Installation photo at the exhibition *January 5–31, 1969*. Exhibition organized and published by Seth Siegelaub. Photo by Seth Siegelaub. Courtesy of The Seth Siegelaub Collection & Archives. © ARS, NY and DACS, London 1997
61 Douglas Huebler *Site Sculpture Project, 50 Mile Piece, Haverhill, Mass. – Putney, Vt. – New York City* 1968. Private collection. Installation photo at the exhibition *January 5–31, 1969*. Exhibition organized and published by Seth Siegelaub. Photo by Seth Siegelaub. Courtesy of The Seth Siegelaub Collection & Archives. © ARS, NY and DACS, London 1997
62 Joseph Kosuth *One and Three Chairs* 1965. Wooden folding chair, photographic copy of a chair, and photographic enlargement of a dictionary definition of a chair; chair 82 x 37.8 x 53 (32⅜ x 14⅞ x 20⅞); photo panel 91.5 x 61.1 (36 x 24⅛); text panel 61 x 61.3 (24 x 24⅛). The Museum of Modern Art, New York. Larry Aldrich Foundation Fund. Photo © 1997 The Museum of Modern Art, New York. © ARS, NY and DACS, London 1997
63 John Baldessari *Everything is purged from this painting but art; no ideas have entered this work* 1966–68. Acrylic on canvas 172.7 x 143.5 (68 x 56½). The Michael and Ileana Sonnabend Collection. Photo courtesy Sonnabend Gallery, New York
64 Robert Barry *All the things I know but of which I am not at the moment thinking – 1:36 pm; June 15, 1969* 1969. Courtesy the artist
65 Terry Atkinson and Michael Baldwin *Map to not indicate* 1967. 50.8 x 62.9 (20 x 24¾). © Tate Gallery, London
66 Art & Language *Index 01* 1972. Eight filing cabinets, forty-eight photostats, and one text in frame. Each cabinet 23 x 29 x 62.5 (9 x 11⅜ x 24⅝); text 75 x 53 (29½ x 20⅞). Private collection. Installed at the exhibition *L'Art Conceptuel, une Perspective*, Musée d'Art Moderne de la Ville de Paris, 22 November 1988 – 18 February 1989. Participating members for this work: Terry Atkinson, David Bainbridge, Michael Baldwin, Ian Burn, Charles Harrison, Harold Hurrell, Joseph Kosuth and Mel Ramsden
67 Dan Graham *Schema* 1966. Private collection, Brussels. Photo Gareth Winters, London. Courtesy Lisson Gallery, London
68 Marcel Broodthaers *Musée – Museum* Ex 73/100 1972. Postcards and ink on paper 50.8 x 74.9 (20 x 29½). Courtesy of Michael Werner Gallery, New York and Cologne
69 Jannis Kounellis *Horses* 1969. Installed at L'Attico Gallery, Rome. Photo courtesy Visual Arts Library, London
70 Giuseppe Penone *Twelve Metre Tree: Ich werde eine Aktion ausführen, die 15 bis 20 Tage dauert. Ich werde ein Holzbrett in die Zeit zurückbringen in der es ein Baum war und zwar in eine Zeit des Baumes, die ich an Ort und Stelle festsetze (I will perform an action which lasts between 15 and 20 days. I will take a plank of wood back to the time when it was a tree and, indeed, to a time whose site and position I will specify)* 1970. Wood 1213 x 25 (477½ x 9⅞). Moderna Museet, Stockholm. © BUS
71 Mario Merz *Igloo de Giap* 1968. Metal, plastic bags, earth H 120 (47¼). Musée National d'Art Moderne, Paris. Photo courtesy Visual Arts Library, London
72 Giovanni Anselmo *Untitled* 1968–86. Granite, lettuce and copper wire 70 x 25 x 25 (27½ x 9⅞ x 9⅞). Private collection. Photo courtesy Visual Arts Library, London
73 Michelangelo Pistoletto *Venus of Rags* 1967. Cement, mica, rags 180 x 130 x 100 (70⅞ x 51⅛ x 39⅜). Collection Peppino di Bernardo, Naples. Photo courtesy Visual Arts Library, London. Photo © G. Colombo, Milan
74 Richard Long *Walking a Line in Peru* 1972. Photograph. Collection of the artist. Courtesy Anthony d'Offay Gallery, London
75 Robert Smithson *Gravel Mirror with Cracks and Dust* 1968. 12 mirrors with gravel 91.4 x 548.6 x 91.4 (36 x 216 x 36). Estate of Robert Smithson, courtesy John Weber Gallery, New York
76 Robert Smithson *Spiral Jetty*, Great Salt Lake, Utah, April 1970. Coil 457.2 m. (1500 ft.) long and approximately 4.57 m. (15 ft.) wide. Black rock, salt crystals, earth, red water (algae). Estate of Robert Smithson, courtesy John Weber Gallery, New York
77 Bernhard and Hilla Becher *Typology of Water Towers* 1972 (detail). Six suites of nine photographs each. Each photograph 40 x 29.8 (15¾ x 11¾); overall 132.4 x 101.8 (52⅛ x $40\frac{1}{16}$). The Eli and Edythe L. Broad Collection, Santa Monica
78 Walter de Maria *Lightning Field* 1971–77. 400 stainless steel poles, with solid stainless steel pointed tips, arranged in a rectangular grid array (16 poles wide by 25 poles long) spaced 67.06 m. (220 ft.) apart, average pole height 6.27 m. (20 ft. 7 in.) but rising to form an even plane. Courtesy Dia Center for the Arts, Corrales, New Mexico. Photo John Cliett, New York
79 Alice Aycock *A Simple Network of Underground Wells and Tunnels*, Merriewold West, Far Hills, New Jersey, 1975. Concrete, wood, earth *c.* 8.53 x 15.24 x 2.74 m. (28 x 50 x 9 ft.), destroyed. Courtesy John Weber Gallery, New York
80 Mary Miss *Untitled*, Battery Park, New York City, 1973. Wood 3.66 x 1.83 m. (12 x 6 ft.); sections at 15.24 m. (50 ft.) intervals. Courtesy the artist
81 Ian Hamilton Finlay with Alexander Stoddart *Apollon Terroriste*, by the Upper Pool, Little Sparta, 1988. Resin and gold leaf. Photo courtesy Ian Hamilton Finlay and Victoria Miro Gallery, London
82 Bruce Nauman *Self-Portrait as a Fountain* 1966–70. Photograph 50.2 x 57.8 (19¾ x 22¾). Photo courtesy Leo Castelli Gallery, New York. © ARS, NY and DACS, London 1997
83 Bruce Nauman *Green Light Corridor* 1970–71. Wallboard and fluorescent light, variable dimensions. Giuseppe Panza di Biumo, Milan. © ARS, NY and DACS, London 1997

84 Dan Graham *Present Continuous Past(s)* 1974. Video camera, video tape, video monitor, mirrors. Musée National d'Art Moderne, Paris. Installed at *Projekt*, Kunsthalle, Cologne, 1974
85 Gilbert & George *Smashed* 1972–73. 10 black-and-white photographs. Overall 124.5 x 132.1 (75 x 52). The Michael and Ileana Sonnabend Collection. Photo courtesy Sonnabend Gallery, New York
86 Vito Acconci *Trappings* 14 October 1971. Performance/installation, Warehouse, Mönchengladbach, Germany. A programme of simultaneous performances. Duration 1 hour. Courtesy Barbara Gladstone Gallery, New York
87 Marina Abramovic *Rhythm 0* 1974. Performed at Studio Mona Gallery, Naples. Duration 6 hours. Courtesy Sean Kelly, New York
88 Joseph Beuys *How to Explain Pictures to a Dead Hare* 1965. Presented at the Galerie Schmela, Düsseldorf. Photo Ute Klophaus, Wuppertal. © DACS 1997
89 Joseph Beuys *Coyote, 'I like America and America likes Me'* 1974. René Block Gallery, New York. Photo Caroline Tisdall. © DACS 1997
90 Leon Golub *Interrogation II* 1981. Acrylic on canvas 304.8 x 426.7 (120 x 168). The Art Institute of Chicago. Gift of the Society for Contemporary Art, 1983.264. Photo © 1996, The Art Institute of Chicago. All Rights Reserved
91 Hans Haacke *Shapolsky et al. Manhattan Real Estate Holdings, a Real-Time Social System, as of May 1, 1971* 1971. 2 maps, 142 black-and-white photographs with typewritten data sheets framed in 23 sets of 6 per frame and 1 set of 4 per frame, 6 charts and explanatory panel (ed. 2). Maps: each 61 x 50.8 (24 x 20); photographs and data sheets: each 50.8 x 19.1 (20 x 7½) (framed sets, 23 at 53.3 x 110.5 [21 x 43½] and one at 54.6 x 76.2 [21½ x 30]); charts: each 61 x 25.4 (24 x 20); panel: 61 x 50.8 (24 x 20). Collection the artist. Photo Hans Haacke. Courtesy John Weber Gallery, New York. © DACS 1997
92 Judy Chicago *The Dinner Party* 1974–79. Mixed media 14.33 x 14.33 x 14.33 m. (47 x 47 x 47 ft.). Photo Michael Alexander, courtesy Through The Flower Corporation
93 Monica Sjoo *God Giving Birth* 1968. Oil on hardboard 183 x 122 (72 x 48). Museum Anna Nordlander, Skellefteå, Sweden. Photo courtesy the artist
94 Eva Hesse *Accession V* 1968. Galvanized steel and rubber tubing 25.4 x 25.4 x 25.4 (10 x 10 x 10). LeWitt Collection, on loan to the Wadsworth Atheneum, Hartford, Connecticut. © Estate of Eva Hesse. Courtesy Robert Miller Gallery, New York
95 Nancy Graves *Paleo-Indian Cave Painting, Southwestern Arizona (To Dr. Wolfgang Becker)* 1970–71. Steel, fibre glass, oil paint, acrylic and 3 wood boards 396.2 x 274.3 x 228.6 (156 x 108 x 90). Neue Galerie der Stadt, Aachen. Sammlung Ludwig. Gift of the artist. Photo Ann Münchow. © Estate of Nancy Graves/DACS, London/VAGA, New York 1997
96 Louise Bourgeois *Fillette* 1968. Latex, L 59.7 (23½). © Louise Bourgeois. Courtesy Robert Miller Gallery, New York
97 Harmony Hammond *Presence IV* 1972. Cloth and acrylic 208.3 x 73.7 x 35.6 (82 x 29 x 14). Collection Best Products, Inc. Photo Dale Anderson
98 Louise Bourgeois *Femme Couteau* 1969–70. Pink marble, L 66 (26). © Louise Bourgeois. Courtesy Robert Miller Gallery, New York
99 Adrian Piper *I Am the Locus #2* 1975. Oil crayon drawing on photograph 20.3 x 25.4 (8 x 10). Courtesy John Weber Gallery, New York
100 May Stevens *Rosa from Prison* from the *Ordinary/Extraordinary* series 1977–80. Mixed media 76.2 x 114.3 (30 x 45). Private collection. Courtesy Mary Ryan Gallery, New York
101 Nancy Spero *Torture of Women* 1976 (detail; panel 10 of 14 panels). Handpainting and typewriter collage on paper 0.51 x 38.1 m. (1 ft. 8 in. x 125 ft.). Courtesy of the Jack Tilton Gallery, New York and P. P. O. W., New York
102 Mary Kelly *Post Partum Document, Documentation VI* 1978–79. 15 slate and resin units, each 35.6 x 27.9 (14 x 11). Arts Council Collection, London
103 Rebecca Horn *Unicorn* 1970–72. Fabric and wood, dimensions variable. Appears in the eponymous film, 1970, and in the film *Performances II* 1973. © DACS 1997
104 Susan Hiller *Dedicated to the Unknown Artists* 1972–76. Postcards, charts and maps mounted on boards; 14 panels, each 69.5 x 109.2 (27⅜ x 43). Installed size variable; book of 56 photographs (*Rough Sea*) and notes. Courtesy the artist
105 Christo (Javacheff) and Jeanne-Claude (de Guillebon) *Wrapped Coast, Little Bay, Australia* 1969. One million square feet of Erosion Control fabric and 36 miles of polypropylene rope. The coast remained wrapped for a period of 10 weeks from 28 October 1969, then all materials were removed and the site returned to its original condition. Copyright Christo 1969. Photo Harry Shunk
106 Maya Ying Lin *Vietnam Veterans Memorial* 1982. Washington Convention and Visitors Association
107 Gordon Matta-Clark *Splitting* 1974. Black-and-white photo-collage 101.6 x 76.2 (40 x 30). Collection of Jane Crawford
108, **109** Exterior and interior views of the Museum of Contemporary Art, Chicago with Michael Asher's work installed, 8 June – 12 August 1979
110 Art & Language *V. I. Lenin by V. Charangovitch (1970) in the Style of Jackson Pollock II* 1980. Enamel and cellulose paint on canvas 239 x 210 (94⅛ x 82⅝). Courtesy Lisson Gallery, London
111 Markus Lüpertz *The Triumph of Line III, 'Monument with Burned Bones'* 1979. Oil and mixed media on canvas 200 x 162 (78¾ x 63¾). Courtesy of Michael Werner Gallery, New York and Cologne. Photo Whitechapel Art Gallery, London
112 Francesco Clemente *The Fourteen Stations, No. III* 1981–82. Encaustic on canvas 198 x 236 (78 x 93). Private collection
113 Georg Baselitz *Finger Painting I – Eagle – à la* 1971–72. Oil on canvas 200 x 130 (78¾ x 51⅛). Neue Galerie, Staatliche und Städtische Kunstsammlungen Kassel, private loan
114 Jörg Immendorff *Eigenlob stinkt nicht* 1983. Oil on canvas 150 x 200 (59 x 78¾). Courtesy of Michael Werner Gallery, New York and Cologne
115 Gerhard Richter *18, Oktober 1977 c.* 1988. Museum Haus Esters 29 April – 4 June 1989. Krefelder Kunstmuseen, Krefeld. © Krefelder Kunstmuseen. Photo Volker Döhne
116 Anselm Kiefer *Margarethe* 1981. Oil and straw on canvas 280 x 380 (110 x 150). Courtesy Anthony d'Offay Gallery, London, by permission of the artist
117 Eric Fischl *Bad Boy* 1981. Oil on canvas 168 x 244 (66 x 96). Private collection
118 Julian Schnabel *Oar: for the one who comes out to know fear* 1981. Oil, crockery, car body filler paste, wood on wood 322.6 x 444.5 x 33 (127 x 175 x 13). Private collection
119 Susana Solano *Thermal Station, No. 1* 1987. Black galvanized iron 132 x 276 x 276 (51½ x 107½ x 107½). Private collection. © DACS 1997
120 Malcolm Morley *SS Amsterdam in Front of Rotterdam* 1966. Acrylic on canvas 157.5 x 213.4 (62 x 84). Private collection
121 Howard Hodgkin *In Bed in Venice* 1984–88. Oil on wood 98.1 x 119.1 (38⅝ x 46⅞). Collection Paine Webber Group, Inc., New York. Photo courtesy the artist
122 Philip Guston *The Studio* 1969. Oil on canvas 121.9 x 106.7 (48 x 42). Private collection. Courtesy McKee Gallery, New York. Photo Eric Pollitzer
123 Leon Kossoff *Christchurch Spitalfields, Morning* 1990. Oil on board 198 x 188.5 (78 x 74½). Tate Gallery, London. Photo Prudence Cumming, London. Courtesy L. A. Louver, Venice, California
124 Tim Rollins and K. O. S. *Amerika VI* 1986–87. Gold watercolour and charcoal on book pages on linen 167.6 x 480.1 (66 x 189). Private collection
125 Jean-Michel Basquiat *Discography two* 1983. Acrylic and oil crayon on canvas 168 x 152 (66⅛ x 59⅞). Courtesy Galerie Bischofberger, Zurich. © ADAGP, Paris and DACS, London 1997
126 Keith Haring *Untitled* September 1983. Chalk on black paper 220.9 x 116.8 (87 x 46). © The Estate of Keith Haring. Used by permission
127 David Wojnarowicz *Sex Series* 1988–89. Black-and-white photograph 78.7 x 86.9 (31 x 34¼). Courtesy of P. P. O. W. Photo Adam Reich
128 Gran Fury *Untitled* 1990. Three billboards. Exhibited at the 1990 Venice Biennale
129 Frank Moore *Arena* 1992. Oil on canvas on wood with frame, overall 155 x 183 (61 x 72). Private collection. Courtesy Sperone Westwater, New York
130 Philip Taaffe *Overtone* 1983. Linoprint, collage, acrylic on paper 225 x 225 (88⅝ x 88⅝). Photo courtesy Galerie Ascan Crone, Hamburg
131 Ashley Bickerton *Le Art (Composition with Logos 2)* 1987. Silkscreen, acrylic lacquer on plywood with aluminium 87.6 x 182.9 x 38.1 (34½ x 72 x 15). Private collection
132 Peter Halley *White Cell with Conduit* 1986. Acrylic, Day-Glo and Roll-a-tex on canvas 147.5 x 285 (58 x 112¼). Private collection

133 Robert Gober *Untitled* 1991. Wood, wax, leather, fabric and human hair 38.7 x 41.9 x 114.3 (15¼ x 16½ x 45). Installed at Galerie Nationale du Jeu de Paume, Paris, 3 October 1991 – 1 December 1991. Courtesy the artist

134 Robert Gober *Double Sink* 1984. Plaster, wood, wire lathe, steel, latex and enamel paint 91.4 x 162.6 x 71.1 (36 x 64 x 28). Private collection

135 Haim Steinbach *related and different* 1985. Plastic laminated wood shelf, leather basketball shoes, brass candlesticks 91 x 52 x 51 (36 x 20½ x 20). Private collection

136 Jeff Koons *One Ball Total Equilibrium Tank* 1985. Glass, iron, water, sodium chloride reagent, basketball 164.5 x 78.1 x 36 (64¾ x 30¾ x 13¼). Private collection

137 Martin Kippenberger *With the Best Intentions I Can't Find a Swastika* 1984. Oil on canvas, 160 x 133 (63 x 52⅜). Courtesy Buro Kippenberger, Galerie Gisela Capitain, Cologne

138 Rosemarie Trockel *Cogito, Ergo Sum* 1988. Wool on canvas 210 x 160 (82⅝ x 63). Courtesy Galerie Monika Sprüth, Cologne

139 Sigmar Polke *Higher Powers Command: Paint the Upper Right Corner Black!* 1969. Lacquer on canvas 150 x 120 (60 x 49). Froehlich Collection, Stuttgart

140 Andreas Gursky *Tokyo* 1990. Cibachrome print 165 x 200 (64.9 x 78.7). Courtesy Galerie Monika Sprüth, Cologne

141 Candida Höfer *Natural History Museum, London II* 1990. Cibachrome print 36 x 52 (14⅛ x 20½). Courtesy Galerie Johnen & Schöttle, Cologne

142 Katharina Fritsch *Tischgesellschaft* (*Company at Table*) 1988. 32 polyester figures, cotton clothes and table cloth, wooden table and benches 140 x 1600 x 175 (55⅛ x 630 x 69). Museum für Moderne Kunst, Frankfurt-am-Main. On permanent loan from the Dresdener Bank, Frankfurt-am-Main. Photo Axel Schneider. © DACS 1997

143 Louise Lawler *How Many Pictures* 1989. Cibachrome print 157.2 x 122.1 (61⅞ x 48). Edition of 5. Courtesy of the artist and Metro Pictures, New York

144 Sherrie Levine *Untitled (After Walker Evans #3, 1936)* 1981. Photograph 25.4 x 20.3 (10 x 8). © Walker Evans Archive, The Metropolitan Museum of Art, New York. Courtesy Mary Boone Gallery, New York

145 Jenny Holzer 'Truism' on T-shirt modelled by Lady Pink 1983. Copyright Barbara Gladstone. Photo courtesy Barbara Gladstone Gallery, New York

146 Cindy Sherman *Untitled Film Still* 1977. Black-and-white photograph 20.3 x 25.4 (8 x 10). Courtesy of the artist and Metro Pictures, New York

147 Richard Serra *Tilted Arc* 1981. Cor-Ten steel 3.66 x 36.58 x 0.06 m. (12 x 120 ft. x 2½ in.). Installed at Federal Plaza, New York. Photo courtesy of PaceWildenstein, New York. © ARS, NY and DACS, London 1997

148 Richard Deacon *Art for Other People No. 10* 1984. Galvanized steel and linoleum 40 x 90 x 90 (15¾ x 35⅜ x 35⅜). Private collection, New York. Courtesy Lisson Gallery, London

149 Reinhard Mucha *The Figure-Ground Problem in Baroque Architecture* (*Das Figur-Grund Problem in der Architektur des Barock* [*für dich allein bleibt nur das Grab*]) 1985. Dodecahedron composed of 2 tiers of superimposed panels (tables) covered in matt grey formica, assembled on an armature of aluminium bars, 8 step ladders and 36 neon lights, stands, partially lacquered glass plate, felt, trolleys raising the work by 17 cm. (6⅝), 12 wooden socles 340 x 450 x 450 DIA 330 (133⅞ x 177⅛ x 177⅛ DIA 130). Musée National d'Art Moderne, Paris

150 Tony Cragg *New Stones – Newton's Tones* 1978. Plastic 330 x 235 (129⅞ x 92½). Arts Council Collection, London. Courtesy Lisson Gallery, London

151 Judith Barry *Echo* 1986. 2 slides, 2 film projections per side of wall which bisects room diagonally, dimensions variable; running time approximately 1 minute; sound track. Commissioned and produced by The Museum of Modern Art, New York. Photo courtesy the artist and Xavier Hufkens Gallery, Brussels

152 Barbara Bloom *The Reign of Narcissism* 1988–89. Installed at Jay Gorney Modern Art, New York, September 1989. Collection of the Museum of Contemporary Art, Los Angeles. Photo courtesy the artist

153 Sylvie Fleury *Poison* 1992. Shopping bags 68.6 x 152.4 x 76.2 (27 x 60 x 30). Courtesy Postmasters Gallery, New York

154 Hans Haacke *Die Freiheit wird jetzt einfach gesponsert – aus der Portokasse (Freedom is now just going to be sponsored – out of petty-cash)* 1990. Exhibited at *Die Endlichkeit der Freiheit*, DAAD, Berlin, 1990. Courtesy John Weber Gallery, New York. Photo Werner Zellien. © DACS 1997

155 Christian Boltanski *The Missing House*, installed at Grosse Hamburger Strasse 15–16, Berlin, 1990. Plaques. Exhibited at *Die Endlichkeit der Freiheit*, DAAD, Berlin, 1990. Photo Werner Zellien. © ADAGP, Paris and DACS, London 1997

156 Rachel Whiteread *House* 1993. Sprayed concrete. Commissioned by Artangel and Beck's. Photo Sue Ormerod, courtesy Artangel

157 Mike Kelley *Dialogue #2 (Transparent White Glass/Transparent Black Glass)* 1991. Blanket, stuffed animals, cassette player 187.9 x 124.5 x 27.9 (74 x 49 x 11). Courtesy the artist and Metro Pictures, New York. Photo © Ellen Page Wilson 1992

158 Simon Patterson *The Great Bear* 1992. Lithograph print 109 x 134.8 x 5 (42⅞ x 53 x 2). Courtesy Lisson Gallery, London. Photo John Riddy, London

159 Damien Hirst *I Wanna Be Me* 1990–91. Old drug bottles in cabinet 137.2 x 101.6 x 22.9 (54 x 40 x 9). Courtesy Jay Jopling, London

160 Andres Serrano *Piss Christ* 1987. Cibachrome print, silicone, plexiglass, wood frame 152.4 x 101.6 (60 x 40). Edition of 4. Courtesy Paula Cooper Gallery, New York

161 Robert Mapplethorpe *Thomas, 1986* 1986. © The Estate of Robert Mapplethorpe/Courtesy A+C Anthology, New York

162 Cheri Samba *Les Capotes utilisées* 1990. Acrylic on canvas 132.1 x 200.7 (52 x 79). Courtesy Annina Nosei Gallery, New York

163 Rasheed Araeen *A Long Walk in the Wilderness* 1991. Old/used shoes. Installed at Vancouver Art Gallery, Vancouver 1991

164 Richard Long *Red Earth Circle* 1989. Installed at *Magiciens de la Terre*, Centre Georges Pompidou, Paris, 18 May – 14 August 1989. Photo courtesy Anthony d'Offay Gallery, London. By permission of the artist, courtesy Anthony d'Offay Gallery, London

165 Adrian Piper *What It's Like, What It Is #3*. Installed at the exhibition *Dislocations*. The Museum of Modern Art, New York. 16 October 1991 – 7 January 1992. Photo © 1997 The Museum of Modern Art, New York

166 David Hammons *Yo–yo* 1991. Mixed media 15.55 x 6.1 x 5.49 m. (51 x 20 x 18 ft.). Installed at 1991 Carnegie International, Pittsburgh. Reproduced with permission of the Carnegie Museum of Art, Pittsburgh. Courtesy of the Jack Tilton Gallery, New York. Photo Richard Stoner, 1991

167 Sophie Calle *Last Seen: A Lady and Gentleman in Black by Rembrandt* 1991. Photograph 241.9 x 154.9 x 1.3 (95¼ x 61 x ½); text 163.2 x 130.8 (64¼ x 51½). Photo courtesy Leo Castelli Gallery, New York

168, 169 Ilya Kabakov *The Toilet* 1992. Installed at *Documenta IX*, Kassel, 1992. Mixed media 3.05 x 11 x 4.17 m. (10 x 36 x 13½ ft.). Photos Bob Lebek (exterior), Dirk Powers (interior). Courtesy Ilya and Emilia Kabakov

170 Tony Oursler *Sexplotter* (from *The Watching*) 1992 (detail). Cloth, plastic, mini video projector, tripod. Courtesy the artist and Metro Pictures, New York

171 Gary Hill *Tall Ships* 1992. Courtesy Barbara Gladstone Gallery, New York

172 Stan Douglas *Hors-champs* 1992. Installed at ICA, London, September – October 1994. 2 black-and-white video projections (featuring G. Lewis, D. Ewart, K. Carter), running time 13 hours, 20 minutes. Photo courtesy David Zwirner, New York

173 Bill Viola *Nantes Triptych* 1992. Video and sound installation. Edition 1: Musée des Beaux-Arts de Nantes, France; edition 2: Tate Gallery, London. Courtesy Anthony d'Offay Gallery, London. Photo Musée des Beaux-Arts de Nantes

174 Sue Williams *The Yellow Painting* 1992. Acrylic and oil on canvas 162.6 x 137.2 (64 x 54). Courtesy Regen Projects, Los Angeles

175 Pepe Espaliú *The Nest* 1993. Painted iron 125 x 65 x 65 (49¼ x 25⅝ x 25⅝). Installed at *Rites of Passage*, Tate Gallery, London, 1995. Fundación Coca-Cola España, Madrid. Photo Marcus Leith/Mark Heathcote

176 Mona Hatoum *Light Sentence* 1992. Wire-mesh lockers, electric motor, timer, light bulb 198 x 185 x 490 (78 x 72⅞ x 192⅞). Photo Billups/Smith. Courtesy Jay Jopling, London

177 Joseph Beuys *Terremoto in Palazzo* (*Earthquake in the Palace*) 1981. Mixed media 500 x 700 (196⅞ x 275½). Installed at *Rites of Passage*, Tate Gallery, London, 1995. Fondazione Amelio, Istituto per l'Arte Contemporanea, Naples. Photo Marcus Leith. © DACS 1997

178 Felix Gonzalez-Torres *'Untitled' (Lover Boy)* 1990. Blue paper, endless copies, ideal height: 19.1 x 73.7 x 58.4 (7½ x 29 x 23). Collection of Andrea Rosen, New York. Courtesy of Andrea Rosen, New York. Photo Peter Muscato

Index

Page numbers in *italic* refer to illustrations